THE WIRE FOX TERRIER

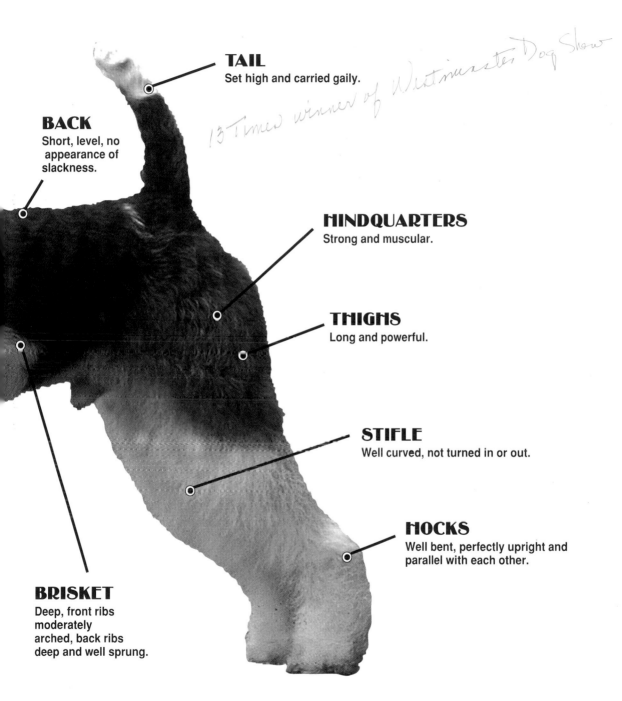

TAIL
Set high and carried gaily.

13 Times winner of Westminster Dog Show

BACK
Short, level, no appearance of slackness.

HINDQUARTERS
Strong and muscular.

THIGHS
Long and powerful.

STIFLE
Well curved, not turned in or out.

HOCKS
Well bent, perfectly upright and parallel with each other.

BRISKET
Deep, front ribs moderately arched, back ribs deep and well sprung.

Title Page: Ch. Galsul Excellence, handled by Peter Green.

Photographers: John L. Ashbey, Caston Studio, Lynn Farr, Isabelle Francais, Chris Halvorson, Jean Mason, Michele Perlmutter, Raymond M. Splawn, Studio One Nineteen, Jane Swanson, C. Wainwright, and Missy Yuhl.

Dedication

This book is dedicated to my tolerant family. Over the years my husband, Jim, has had to play the role of mother to our two daughters, kennel 'boy', whelper, a shoulder to cry on, and provider of understanding (but not always acceptance!) of my need to express myself through the art and sport of purebred dogs. And to Joli and Lori, our daughters, my gratitude for being the "nutrition experts" to my kennel of dogs. And also, my apology for always being away at a dog show on Mother's Day, Senior Prom night, or for tying up the phone when they so badly needed it— and for loving me anyway!

© by T.F.H. Publications, Inc.

Distributed in the UNITED STATES to the Pet Trade by T.F.H. Publications, Inc., One T.F.H. Plaza, Neptune City, NJ 07753; distributed in the UNITED STATES to the Bookstore and Library Trade by National Book Network, Inc. 4720 Boston Way, Lanham MD 20706; in CANADA to the Pet Trade by H & L Pet Supplies Inc., 27 Kingston Crescent, Kitchener, Ontario N2B 2T6; Rolf C. Hagen Inc., 3225 Sartelon St. Laurent-Montreal Quebec H4R 1E8; in CANADA to the Book Trade by Vanwell Publishing Ltd., 1 Northrup Crescent, St. Catharines, Ontario L2M 6P5 ; in ENGLAND by T.F.H. Publications, PO Box 15, Waterlooville PO7 6BQ; in AUSTRALIA AND THE SOUTH PACIFIC by T.F.H. (Australia), Pty. Ltd., Box 149, Brookvale 2100 N.S.W., Australia; in NEW ZEALAND by Brooklands Aquarium Ltd. 5 McGiven Drive, New Plymouth, RD1 New Zealand; in Japan by T.F.H. Publications, Japan—Jiro Tsuda, 10-12-3 Ohjidai, Sakura, Chiba 285, Japan; in SOUTH AFRICA by Lopis (Pty) Ltd., P.O. Box 39127, Booysens, 2016, Johannesburg, South Africa. Published by T.F.H. Publications, Inc.

MANUFACTURED IN THE
UNITED STATES OF AMERICA
BY T.F.H. PUBLICATIONS, INC.

WIRE FOX TERRIER

A COMPLETE AND RELIABLE HANDBOOK

by Ann D. Hearn

RX-100

CONTENTS

CHARACTERISTICS OF THE WIRE FOX TERRIER 7

HISTORY OF THE WIRE FOX TERRIER 9
The Wire Fox Terrier in the United States • The Wire Fox
Terrier Today • The Westminster Kennel Club •
Montgomery County Kennel Club • The Wire Fox Terrier Club
of the Central States

THE STANDARD OF THE WIRE FOX TERRIER 31

SELECTING A WIRE FOX TERRIER 49

YOUR PUPPY'S NEW HOME 53
On Arriving Home • Dangers in the Home • The First Night •
Other Pets • Housetraining • The Early Days • Identification

GROOMING A WIRE FOX TERRIER 65

FEEDING YOUR WIRE FOX TERRIER 73
Factors Affecting Nutritional Needs • Composition and
Role of Food • Amount to Feed • When to Feed

TRAINING YOUR WIRE FOX TERRIER 81
Collar and Leash Training • The Come Command
The Sit Command • The Heel Command • The Stay Command
The Down Command • Recall to Heel Command
The No Command

CHARACTERISTICS OF THE WIRE FOX TERRIER

If you take good care of your Wire Fox Terrier he will live a full, active life and bring much joy to your home.

The life expectancy of a Wire is quite long— approximately 12 to 14 years, depending on the quality of life you provide for him. Nutritious food, daily clean water, weekly grooming sessions to assess the physical health of the dog, and disease preventive vaccinations given on a timely basis are all steps necessary to achieve a healthy and happy pet.

There is no more loyal animal in the world than a dog, and a Wire Fox Terrier tops that list in this characteristic. If it becomes necessary, the breed will die for its master. The joy and vitality a Wire Fox Terrier adds to your home and life is immeasurable, and will bring you years of comfortable camaraderie, sport and love.

MAKE AND SHAPE

It is believed that devout terrier people are of a different mind-set than other dog people. Once a terrier person, always a terrier person, and all other breeds are evaluated against the mental image of the clean, defined outlines of a terrier. There is a strong sisterly kinship among terrier people, but one must earn this respect. The Wire Fox Terrier is one of the most elegant breeds on the American Kennel Club approved list of breeds, with his white body, evening jacket coat of black or tan, smart tail gaily wagging his pride, head up, ears alert and dark eyes darting everywhere and seeing everything. He knows when to be cuddly and when to be tenacious, and when to be a suave gentleman. His sense of smell is uncanny, his vision misses nothing in any direction, and his attitude of eager readiness makes him a dog of worthy substance, and intelligence. He is protective of his home and family, clean, and lovingly loyal to the end.

It is not unusual to find Wires in public advertisements on television and magazines. One of the most renowned stars in the 40s and 50s was the little Wire Fox Terrier in *The Thin Man* series of movies and television. This popular series was the story of a detective husband and wife team, Nick and Nora Charles, who always included the wily and clever assistance of "Asta," their pet Wire.

The Wire is a breed that requires a firm hand in his upbringing, a coat that necessitates particular care, and a fenced area for his and other predator's benefit. The devotion he will give in return is well worth any amount of time spent on his behalf.

Wire Fox Terriers are well suited for just about anything. They have versatile personalities, a keen sense of smell, vast intelligence, and an eager attitude. Welwyre's Tessie Truehart, owned by Harry and Darlene Welsh.

THE HISTORY OF THE WIRE FOX TERRIER

The Wire Fox Terrier was developed in England and recognized as a breed around the 1500s. Ch. SunnyBrook Spot On, handled by Peter Green.

Elegant, intelligent, loyal to family, and daring—these are words describing the Wire Fox Terrier. The American Kennel Club recognizes two Fox Terrier breeds. One is the Wire, which refers to the hair type, and the other is the Smooth coat. Sisters by virtue of early lineage, they do not have as many similarities as they once did.

An English dog, bred from the original white terrier combined with the rough coated black-and-tan terrier, the Fox Terrier was developed for hunting and was recognized around the late 1500s. He was small enough to go into a hole in the ground burrowed by a fox, badger or ferret, snatch them in his teeth, and then back out of the hole with the critter in tow, thus ridding the farmer of troublesome vermin. Good looks were not the criteria when breeding these early dogs— but the ability to work was the priority. In some areas of England the Fox Terrier ran in the hunt along with the hounds. The Fox Terrier was a valuable asset to both huntsman and farmer, earning his keep as well as a place in history.

The Latin word "terra" means earth. Therefore, this underground, small dog was aptly named Terrier. Absolute authenticity concerning the progression of the Wire is fairly obscure, however there are numerous pieces of early 16th and 17th century art showing a small rough coated white dog with a pattern of color on his coat. There is written mention of the Wire Fox Terrier as early as 1677 in *Gentleman's Recreation*, authored by Nicholas Cox, where he states, "There are two sorts of Terriers — one with legs more or less crooked and with short coats while the other are straighter in leg and have long jackets…" Because the terrier was used to a great extent as a hunter there is

Opposite: The exact development of the Wire Fox Terrier is not known, but there are pieces of art work dating from the 16th and 17th century showing a small, rough coated dog with colors on his coat that resemble the Wire Fox Terrier. Raylu puppy, owned by Gene Bigelow.

The Latin word "terra" means earth—hence, the name of this underground, small dog. This puppy is learning to "go-to-ground."

frequent mention of his likeness to the hound. John Marvin, in *The Book of All Terriers*, quotes Oliver Goldsmith in 1774, who states that a terrier without "voice" is not much of a worker. "The terrier is a small kind of hound, with rough hair, made use of to force the fox and badger out of their holes; or rather to give notice by their barking in what part of their kennel the fox or badger resides, when the sportsmen intend to dig them out." Frequently the terrier drove the varmint out of the hole into the waiting nets of the hunter.

The mention of "crooked" legs is evidence that terriers like the Scottish, West Highland White, Cairn— all of bent front legs—have much the same lineage and usefulness as the straight-legged terriers such as the Airedale, Irish, Wire and Smooth Fox. It has been suggested in the readings of old that the bent-legged "terrars" were better at digging while in the hole, because the dirt was thrown backward between those outwardly bent legs, allowing the front end to do its work, and thus the dog was never boxed in. However, in defense of the Fox Terrier type, George Turbeville (1540-1610) wrote in his book, *The Noble Arte of*

Wire Fox Terriers are known throughout history as working dogs. Oftentimes, they were used to drive varmint out of their holes into the waiting net of a hunter.

Opposite: Ch. Crystcrack Fox Trot, CD, owned by Audrey S. Brown.

Venerie or Hunting, published in 1575, the following:

"Of the Huntinge of the Foxe and Badgerd

Now to speak of Foxe hounds and Terryers, and how you should enter them to take the Foxe, the Badgerd, and suche like vermine: you muste understand that there are sundrie sortes of Terriers, whereof wee hold opinion that one sorte came out of Flaunders or the low countries, as Artoys and thereabouts, and they have crooked legges, and are shorte heared moste commonly. Another sorte there is which are shagged and streight legged: those with the crooked legges will take earth better than the other, and are better for the Badgerd, bycause they will lye longer at a vermine: but the others with streyght legges do serve for two purposes, for they wyll Hunte above grounde as well as other houndes, and enter the earthe with more furie than the others: but they will not abide so long, bycause they are too eagre in fight, and therefore are constreyned to come out to take the ayre: there are both good and badde of bothe sortes."

It was the appeal of the terrier not only as an exuberant, outdoor, working dog, but also as an indoor, willing, and adoring pet, that clinched the future of the terriers.

A review of the many oil paintings, stories, poems, and writings of those early days will not and can not provide a specific date when the Fox Terrier left the all encompassing group called "terryer" and went its own way to be recognized today by its definitive breed name. Obviously it was a situation where the region encouraged a different look and structure to fit the needs—the topography of the country dictating those needs, i.e.: rocky, mountainous, pasture, etc. There were efforts by early breeders to develop other types of terriers that proved unsuccessful and have fallen into obscurity because of lack of popularity, which added a determining dimension to the creation of the beautiful terriers that are recognized today.

The admission of the bulldog-type dog into the development and pedigrees of the terrier has merit, for it was in those early days that Bulldogs were used to constrain the bulls, latch onto the animal with their great mouth, and with tenacity and unbelievable strength, would fight the bull into obedience. That determination is still prevalent in Wire Fox Terriers today—but not so in Bulldogs.

In 1815 Sir Walter Scott wrote of a specific breed, the Dandie Dinmont Terrier, in his touching novel

Opposite: A review of all the paintings and writings of the early days can not provide a specific date when the Wire Fox Terrier left the all encompassing "terryer" group and went his own way. Ch. Berylean Eclipse, owned by Raylu Kennels and The McKennas.

called *Guy Mannering*. This is the story of the ultimate devotion of a little terrier to his master. In the 19th century, the breeds began to develop specific physical attributes, and were eventually categorized, then bred with focus on each ultimate type. The first English dog show was held at Newcastle-on-Tyne, England in June 1859 with classes for hunting dogs. Fox Terriers were allowed to be entered in the Miscellaneous Class the following year. Fourteen years later the English Kennel Club was founded. In 1862, Wire Fox Terriers, known as Rough Haired Terriers, were shown in Birmingham, England in the Miscellaneous Class, and in 1879 they were finally recognized and allowed to be shown in their individual breed classification. In 1882, the English Kennel Club registry changed the classification to "Wire-Haired Fox Terriers." The Fox Terrier Club of England was formed in 1876, and the standard for the varieties (both coats) was drawn at this time. So well written, it was recognized and acclaimed by the American Fox Terrier Club, and remained the criteria until the Smooth and Wire Fox Terrier breeds were divided into two separate breeds in 1986.

Opposite: Wire Fox Terriers were finally recognized and allowed to be shown in their individual breed classification in 1879, Ch. Raylu Recharge ROM, owned by Gene Bigelow.

A promising Wire Fox Terrier pup can be anything you desire: a champion, companion dog, therapy dog, and more—but definitely a best friend!

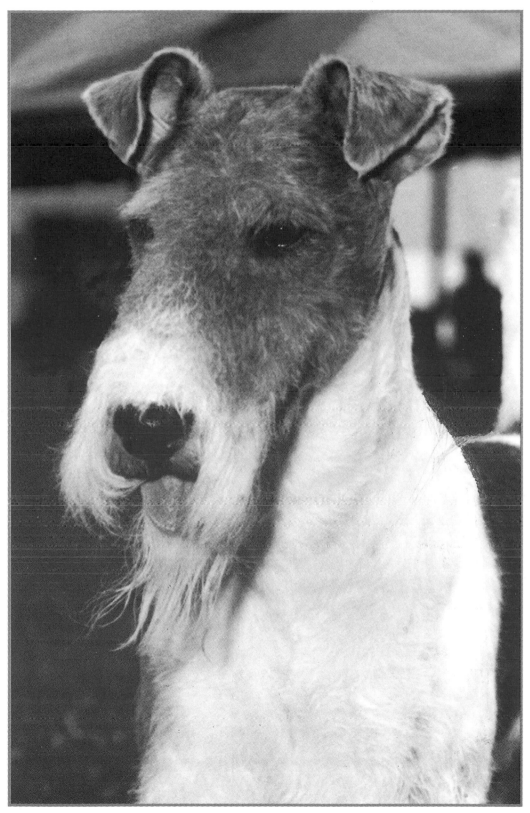

The Fox Terrier Club was formed in 1876. The standard for both Wire and Smooth Fox Terriers was drawn, and remained the criteria until the separation of the two breeds in 1986.

With the dawning of official dog shows that require cataloging and record keeping, the path of pedigree development of Wire Fox Terriers becomes easier to follow. There are many key people in those early days of merry old England we can thank for building and protecting the Wire type, and who shared their bloodlines with friends across the pond. In England, Her Grace, the Duchess of Newcastle was a top breeder and judge, and had many winning dogs including Ch. Cackler of Notts. No listing of old important kennels and breeders would be complete without noting Sir Frances Redman who bred both Wires (Dusky) and Smooths (Totteridge). Also, we acknowledge R. Phillips (Banwen), F. Pearse (Barrington) who bred the vastly valuable Ch. Barrington Bridegroom, Mrs. T. Losco Bradley (Cromwell), A. A. W. Simmonds (Epping), Miss M.E. Lewis (Paignton) whose bitches will be found in many of the old pedigrees, W. H. Oldershaw (Olcliffe), F. Calvert Butler (Watteau of both Wire and Smooth fame), and his daughter, Mrs. Mary Blake, who continues the Watteau famous breeding program that appears in today's Smooth pedigrees. We will see future top American-winning dogs from the famous Talavera Kennel of Capt. H. R.

Phipps, J. R. Barlow (Crackley) who gave start to the Wildoaks Kennel in America, Mr. A. Churchill (Weltona), J. Smith (Florate), J. W. Turner (Wycollar), and Mr. W. G. Mitchell (Kirkmoor) who co-bred one of the most splendid dogs to be imported to America, Ch. Gosmore Kirkmoor Coachman. Coachman's fame was enhanced when he produced Ch. Bev-Wyre's Conbrio Tim, a dog who figures in many American pedigrees. English kennel names prominent in the background of top American winners and producers also include Mrs. E. L. Williams (Penda), Mrs. E. Pinkett (Falstaff), Mr. E. Robinson (Zeloy), and A. B. Dallison (Gosmore).

Likewise, there are specific dogs whose type has endured through the years, and whose genes have stamped that type for the future. The first dog imported to America and shown in New York in 1883 was Jack Granger's Tyke from the English Carrick Kennels, and the breed was given recognition on that same momentous day.

Once official dog shows became popular, requiring cataloging and written records, the path of pedigree development for the Wire Fox Terrier becomes easier to discern. Crystcrack Victoria, Crystcrack Tigerlily CD, Ch. Crystcrack Royal Crown CD, and Ch. Raylu Donde Sue, owned by Gloria and Kim Snellings.

THE WIRE FOX TERRIER IN THE UNITED STATES

The first Wire Fox Terrier to be registered by the American Kennel Club was Broxten Virago owned by R. W. Dean of Canada, and is described as "badger-pie head, black patch on left side, white body." It would be difficult to present a head on a Wire Fox Terrier as perfect as the lovely bitch, Virago. Meersbrook Bristles, imported in 1899, was a dog that vastly improved the

breed in head type. He was owned by Mr. Charles Keyes of Boston from the Hillcrest prefix. An interesting fact about Bristles— he was successful in producing important Smooths and Wires and added much to the future of both varieties. Honorable George Steadman Thomas of Endcliffe Kennels, bred refinement into the Wire to the great appeal of the American public. It is to him that the Wire populace is indebted for presenting a dog of such beauty and class.

Many early American breeders who had the foresight to import quality Wire Fox Terriers and then develop their own strain should be recognized. They include Mrs. Richard Bondy (Wildoaks), Forest Hall (Hallwyre Kennels), and Mr. and Mrs. Tom Carruthers, III (Hetherington Kennels) whose lineage can be recognized in many pedigrees of today. Other greats in later years include Mrs. E. A. Kraft (Wynwyre Kennels), Mr. and Mrs. Harold Florsheim (Harham Kennels), Mrs. Joseph W. Urmston (Trucote Ken-

Opposite: Many thanks are owed to the early American breeders of Wire Hair Fox Terriers who imported quality dogs and developed their own strain. One such breeder was Gene Bigelow of Raylu Kennels. Pictured here is Raylu's Donde Bob.

The first Wire Fox Terrier imported and shown in the United States was in 1883 in New York. From then on the breed has continued to gain popularity and recognition. Ch. Sunspryte Peterkins Pepper and Ch. Libner Lad of Welwyre, owned by Harry and Darlene Welsh.

nels), Dr. Charlotte Jones and Evelyn Stark (Koshare Kennels), Mrs. Paul M. Silvernail (Crack-Dale Kennels), Mrs. Barbara W. Keenan (Wishing Well), Mrs. Gene Scaggs Bigelow (Raylu Kennels), Mrs. Franklin Koehler (Merrybrook Kennels), Mrs. Frederick Dutcher (Copper Beech Kennels), and Mr. and Mrs. Thomas M. Gately (Gayterry).

HISTORY

The Wire Fox Terrier world of today has many valuable and deeply devoted breeders. One in particular who has spread style, quality, type and personality generously in the Wire Fox Terrier world is Mrs. Eve Ballich (Evewire Kennels) of Maryland who has embraced and loved the Wire since 1957. She has bred 110 champions under the Evewire prefix, mostly handled by her. Mrs. Ballich has stated: "The best dog I ever had was Ch. Evewire Druid Dynamic, but Ch. Evewire You Better Believe It, a male, was the most enjoyable because top handler, Peter Green, showed him". One can spot an "Evewire" dog at a glance— they are true to type. Others contributing to today's breed quality include Mari Morrisey (Brookhaven Wires), Virginia Matanic (Briarlea Kennels), Ruth Cooper (Cottleston Kennel), Peter and Gaynor Green

Ch. O'Ryles Irisheyes R. Smiling, CD, CGC, Masons One Over Par Bogey, UD, and Bogey's Little Sundance Miss, CD, owned by Jean Mason.

(Greenfield Kennel), Carol Wainwright (Halcar Kennels), Kathleen Reges (Kathrich Kennel), Sue and Thomas Yates (Mystwyre Kennels), and Bill and Taffe McFadden of California (Random Kennels), who have produced and are handlers of top dogs of all breeds. Others include: Mr. and Mrs. Raymond Splawn (Wyrequest Kennels), Mr. and Mrs. Wayne Bousek (Bowyre), Mr. and Mrs. Richard J. Forkel (Wendywyre), Mrs. Marilyn Laschinski (Aljamar), Mr. and Mrs. Robert Libner (Libwyre), Mr. and Mrs. Myron Hook (Mountain Ayre), Mrs. Carol Wainwright (Halcar), Ms Nancy Lee Wolf (Wyrelee), Mr. and Mrs. James H. Brown (Lynnwyre), Mr. Harold Shook (Halsho), Mr. &

Ch. Halcar Himself, and Ch. Halcar Sea Urchin, GG, CGC, owned by Jean Hale. Winners of Best Breed in Brace at the Montgomery County Kennel Club show.

Mrs. Wood Wornall (Crizwood), Mr. and Mrs. Richard Vida (Foxcreek), Mr. Alton J. Pertuit, Jr. (Fyrewyre), Mr. & Mrs. Jack P. DeWitt (Rhapsodale), Mrs. Irene Rhodes (Foxglen), Ms. Judy Thill (Dubwyre), Mr. & Mrs. Aubrey D. Clay (Deewyre), Ms. Sharon Fitzgerald (El-Ray), Mr. & Mrs. Darrell E. Jorgensen (Ana-Dare), Mrs. Virginia S. Simms (Mountaineer), Mr. & Mrs. Robert H. Fine (Finewyre), Mr. William F. Johnson (Fairfield), Mrs. Merrilee Henderson (Cedarbriar), Dr. S. P. & Peggy Beisel McIlwaine (Foxairn), and Mr. & Mrs. George Ward (Albany). George Ward has imported, conditioned, and handled some of the top terriers in this country and is the epitomy of "a dog man." He and his wife, Roz, are considered the premier couple in presentation of a wire coat. If you want your dog to be presented to its maximum, to be cared for impeccably, then send him to George and Roz with the knowledge that he is in capable hands.

The Santeric Wires with Richard Chashoudian at the helm, have been developed through the eye of an artist, judge, professional handler, and ardent breeder. Mr. Chashoudian of Louisiana was one of the top professional dog handlers, with terriers being his specialty. He has used his knowledge to specifically illustrate his view of a terrier by sculpting them in bronze, and is now highly regarded as a judge and artisan. His pieces of sculpture are treasured by owners fortunate enough to obtain one. However, breeding, his original commitment, continues to be a part of his life.

WIRE FOX TERRIERS TODAY

A clear example for the student of proper Wire head piece, and one that completely reveals the delicate nuances of proper type and grooming, must include one of my favorite and all-time most impressive Wire bitches—Ch. Gaines Great Surprise of Wildoaks out of Ch. Talavera Simon and New Town Bella Donah. Surprise was a totally white-bodied bitch, with perfect markings on her head. Her value to the breed is recognized in her highly successful progeny.

Ch. Sunspryte's Disco "Dolly" and her Welsh Terrier friend , Ch. Xxtra Sunspryte of El-Fri-Ba, owned by Carole Beattie, enjoying the view.

The mark of a great dog is not necessarily his show credits, but whether he or she can consistently produce successful progeny.

There have been so many beautiful Wires shown in the ring it would be difficult to list all, however there are some that have made such a dynamic impact on the breed they must be acknowledged: Ch. Woolsack Evening Flirt, Ch. Crackley Supreme of Wildoaks, Ch. Gallant Fox of Wildoaks, Gallant Knight of Wildoaks, Ch. Mac's Revelation, Ch. Deko Druid, Ch. Evewire Little Man, Ch. Evewire Druid Dynamic, Ch. Evewire Exemplar, Ch. Evewire You Better Believe It, Ch. Talludo Minstrel of Purston, Eng. Am. Ch. Sunnybrook Spot On, and his son, Ch. Aryee Dominator. All-breed top winner for 1977 was Eng. Am. Ch. Harwire Hetman of Whinlatter, who was a terrific dog. Also, Ch. Denidale Olga of Halsho, Ch. Sylair Special Edition, Ch. Cunningfox Santeric Patriot, Ch. Louline Peterman, Ch. Louline Stringalong. Last, but certainly not least is Ch. Galsul Excellence—a dynamite dog who was creating a record in producing typy Wires when his career was cut short due to legalities. "Paddy" went Best in Show at Montgomery County, and in 1986 was Show Dog of the Year. A dog or bitch that can produce nice puppies is a great value to a breeding kennel, but a dog or bitch that can consistently produce quality, productive, top-winning bitches is worth ten times her weight in gold. Paddy produced the lovely bitch, Ch. Registry's Lonesome Dove who won at the Westminster Kennel Club. Another of Mr.

Chashoudian's beautiful home-bred bitches who sired Ch. Santeric's Stormin Norman, was Ch. Santeric's Fleur De Lee. From the Raylu line of Gene Bigelow, and from whom I ultimately got my start in Wires, comes Ch. Raylu Replica, Ch. Raylu Raconteur, and Ch. Raylu Recharge. Also, there was Can. Am. Ch. Wyrequest Pay Dirt, and from Hawaii came one of the loveliest Wire bitches, Eng. Am. Ch. Blackdale Queen of Dreams. Queenie was handled by Susan Kipp who manages to successfully juggle being super mom, handler extraordiniare, and beautiful conditioner of dogs. There are literally hundreds more Wires that should be mentioned, that are not only beautiful, strong producers, but who also have acquired note-worthy wins but it would be impossible to list them all.

WESTMINSTER KENNEL CLUB

Who knows? Maybe one of these young Wire pups will be a champion at the prestigious Westminster Kennel Club Dog Show some day.

The prestigious Westminster Kennel Club, holds its shows at Madison Square Garden in New York City during the month of February. This nationally televised,

splendid, two-day dog show is the show-of-all-shows, with distinguished judges elegantly dressed in long gowns and tuxedos. The week of Westminster provides an opportunity to attend many fancy parties, dog related seminars, specialty breed events, and award recognition dinners. This show summons dog enthusiasts from all over the world. Due to the over-abundant participation, entries are

The Westminster Kennel Club Dog Show is a two day event held in New York City. Considered the pinnacle of all dog shows, entries are limited to champions only.

now exclusive to champions only. The Wire Fox Terrier has been amply recognized with top awards at this celebrated event, and is considered by many to be the pinnacle of achievement for the breeder, owner, and handler. Indeed, to win Best of Breed at this creme de la creme competition is an honor to treasure for a lifetime. The first Wire Fox Terrier to win at Westminster was in 1915 when George W. Quintard's Ch. Matford Vic went Best in Show, which he achieved again in 1916. A Wire won the show again in 1917 and 1920 by the name of Ch. Conejo Wycollar Boy, who was owned by Mrs. Roy A. Rainey. In 1926 the famed Halleston Kennels won with Ch. Signal Circuit of Halleston. Ch. Talavera Margaret, owned by R. M. Lewis went BIS in 1928, and in 1930 and 1931, Ch. Pendley Calling of Blarney owned by John G. Bates won. Continuing the Wire Fox Terrier record for top wins at Madison Square Garden, in 1934 the Halleston Kennels won with Ch. Flornell Spicy Bit of Halleston and again in 1937 with Ch. Flornell Spicey Piece of Halleston, who was closely related to Spicy Bit. In 1946, Mr. and Mrs. T.H. Carruthers, III won with Ch. Heatherington Model Rhythm who is said to have been a racy bitch, very flashy, all white except for her ears and one eye, and was a litter sister of Ch. Heatherington Navy Nurse, who was also a top winner during that time. Navy Nurse had more bone and was a well-bodied bitch. In

1966, Ch. Zeloy Mooremaide's Magic won, owned by Marion G. Bunker, and was one of the most gorgeous coated bitches, with lovely reach of neck. Ric Chashoudian has stated that Magic "was the best Wire Fox Terrier I had seen." He also feels we were very fortunate to have had access to bloodlines from the great Zeloy Emporer, Magic's sire, as he was dominant for producing great heads. Ric further states that Magic had beautiful movement, a lovely head piece, wonderful temperament, and a gorgeous jacket.

The Montgomery County Kennel Club show began in 1929 as a specialty for terriers only. It is an annual celebration that attracts terrier students from all over the world. Maybe this pup will appear there someday.

Not until 1992 did a Wire Fox Terrier reclaim that prestigious Best In Show ribbon, with a bitch owned by Marion and Samuel Lawrence and bred by her handler, Michael Kemp. This was the lovely Ch. Registry's Lonesome Dove.

MONTGOMERY COUNTY KENNEL CLUB

George Frank Skelly, in his book *All About Fox Terriers*, recognized the true meaning of the sport of showing dogs, and stated: "Dog shows, as most breeders recognize, are designed primarily for the purpose of selecting the better breeding specimens and only secondarily as a sporting contest. Hence, in both theory and practice, a Wire fancier's success is best measured by ability to breed Wires of championship caliber." How true—words we must live by for all eternity.

And so it was that in 1926 a group of terrier people from an AKC member club named Gwynedd Valley Kennel Club met to formulate an all-terrier club and event. The Wissahickon Kennel Club was a part of this development, and they provided shows for terriers only. The cooperative efforts of individuals involved in all three organizations began a tradition they could not know would become the culmination of all terrier stardom in the US. And so, the terrier world, a close-knit, family-minded group of people, held its first Montgomery County Kennel Club show in 1929, for terrier breeds only. The annual celebration of this event has attracted terrier students from Japan, Aus-

Ch. Welwyre's Spiced Pepper, owned by Harry and Darlene Welsh at the Montgomery County Kennel Club dog show.

tralia, Russia, Sweden and all parts of the world to attend its show now held in Ambler, Pennsylvania. Most terrier breed clubs consider this show a Specialty, and provide a Sweepstakes competition for young dogs. The show culminates with a Best Brace in Show, and finally with the ultimate Best in Show — a top specimen chosen from the various breed winners. To have one's entry acknowledged with even a placement at this show is memorable. To be invited to judge this event is the highest of honors. Wires have held their own at Montgomery County with Best In Show being awarded eight times to the "gentlemen's" terrier, including the first show in 1929.

WIRE FOX TERRIER CLUB OF THE CENTRAL STATES

Motivated by the extreme emphasis being placed on the Smooth Fox Terrier in the early 40s, lovers of the Wire variety attempted to equalize the trend. A group of supporters of the Wire appealed to the parent club, The American Fox Terrier Club, for recognition to hold a Wire Fox Terrier-only event, but were met with resistance. They decided to form an association called the Wire Fox Terrier Club, and met in 1945 with more than 100 members. They held a specialty in November 1946 in Chicago. In 1947, the group made repeated attempts to hold a sanctioned specialty, but they continued to be ignored, stating the territory claimed by the club was in conflict. The American Kennel Club backed the AFTC and limited the territory where their shows could be held. Thus the name was changed to The Wire Fox Terrier Club of the Central States that encompassed a territory acceptable to AKC and AFTC, with 1996 marking the 50th anniversary. While all dog shows enable breeders and exhibitors to study and exchange ideas, the Central States focuses specifically on the intricacies of the Wire. Top handlers, breeders, and students of the Wire Fox Terrier faithfully make this annual trip to Cincinnati in May.

In 1946, The Wire Hair Fox Terrier Club was formed. Their purpose is to provide an opportunity for breeders and exhibitors to gather and discuss the Wire Hair Fox Terrier development.

THE STANDARD OF THE WIRE FOX TERRIER

The AKC first approved a written standard for the Wire Fox Terrier in 1876. This is Ch. Cedarbriar's Autumn Cheviot, owned by Jack and Robin Pensinger.

The American Kennel Club approved a written standard in 1876 for the Wire Fox Terrier. Proposed by its breed defending denizens from the written guidelines of the English Kennel Club it was also adopted by the American Fox Terrier Club. In reading the standard one must appreciate the writing style of the authors of years ago. Following each section is the author's explanation in italics. Any deviation from the statements in the Standard is not acceptable.

GENERAL APPEARANCE

The terrier should be alert, quick of movement, keen of expression, on the tip-toe of expectation at the slightest provocation. Character is imparted by the expression of the eyes and by the carriage of ears and tail.

Bone and strength in a small compass are essential, but this must not be taken to mean that a Terrier should be "cloddy," or in any way coarse—speed and endurance being requisite as well as power. The Terrier must on no account be leggy, nor must he be too short on the leg. He should stand like a cleverly made, short-backed hunter, covering a lot of ground.

N.B. Old scars or injuries, the result of work or accident, should not be allowed to prejudice a Terrier's chance in the show ring, unless they interfere with its movement or with its utility for work or stud.

The words used to describe a Wire Fox Terrier should conjure up an image that provides the essence of the dog—the attitude, expectations, and where one might look to affirm these qualities. To even casually consider the Wire as soft, easy-going, laid-back, quietly and complacently sleeping at your feet, would be out of character. Instead, the Wire is full of fun, spirit and ready for a romp in rain, shine, mud, sleet or snow. He will never let you down, and will always be ever-ready for any undertaking you can perceive. In the Wire Fox Terrier, alert is synonymous with anticipatingly eager. This is not a large breed nor is it small like a Toy breed, but it is an ideal size for home, apartment, travel, and due to their tenacity and bravery, they provide excellent protection for the family. They fear nothing, and will attack a dog the size of a Great Dane, a bear, or a mole as easily and quickly as needed to fend for their loved ones. I mention a mole and share a true story with you. Early one spring we found that a mole was burrowing through our back yard and no matter what we did, Mr. Mole was there to stay and demolish our stand of grass, eat the flowering bulbs, and threaten the roots of the young trees. Lynda, one of our champion Wire's, watched with growing concern as we attempted repeatedly to rid our yard of this pest. One day on her own, Lynda decided enough-was-enough and with a "hard-bitten eye" determination "took to earth" after the rodent. She unearthed him, wrestled with him, and made quick work in completing the task we were unable to do. She lost a toe in the invasion, and proudly bore her wound to us for praise.

Size, Proportion, Substance—According to present-day requirements, a full-sized, well balanced dog should not exceed 15 ¹/₂ inches at the withers— the bitch being proportionately lower—nor should the length of back from withers to root of tail exceed 12 inches, while to maintain the relative proportions, the head—as mentioned below— should not exceed 7 ¹/₄ inches or be less than 7 inches. A dog with these measurements should scale 18 pounds in show condition—a bitch weighing some two pounds less—with a margin of one pound either way.

The dog should be balanced and this may be defined as the correct proportions of a certain point or points, when considered in relation to a certain other point or points. It is the key-stone of the terrier's anatomy. The chief points for consideration are the relative proportions of skull and foreface; head and back; height at withers; and length of body from shoulder-point to buttock — the ideal of proportion being reached when the last two measurements are the same. It should be added that, although the head measurement can be taken with absolute accuracy, the height at withers and length of back are approximate, and are inserted for the information of breeders and exhibitors rather than as a hard-and-fast rule.

Wire Fox Terriers can only become show dogs when they are good examples of the breed standard. Wyrequest's Zip Code, owned by Mr. and Mrs. Splawn.

STANDARD

A Wire Fox Terrier is a square dog. It is as simple as that. Whether looking at a puppy of eight weeks or an adult dog, you should see a square body, with a prideful, upright head and neck at one end and the tail pointing up from the other. The legs should approximate the body depth, thereby providing a look of balance, i.e.: the body being the same up and down as it is front to end, with legs of the same measurement. The tail is docked to a length that balances with the neck and head, thus giving a completeness and orderly look to the dog. Even though the Fox Terrier is a very old breed that dates back at least to the early 14th century, one envisions the clean, clear lines of Biedermeir modern furniture, as opposed to the soft, cushiony comfort of traditional design.

An important consideration when selecting a Wire is balance. Are all the parts of the dog in proportion to one another? Ch. Sunspryte's Prime Contender, owned by Carole Beattie.

Head—The length of the *head* of a full-grown, well-developed dog of correct size—measured with calipers—from the back of the occipital bone to the nostrils—should be from 7 to 7 ¼ inches, the bitch's head being proportionately shorter. Any measurement in excess of this usually indicates an over-sized or long-backed specimen, although occasionally—so rarely as to partake of the nature of a freak—a Terrier of correct size may boast a head 7 ½ inches in length. In a well-balanced head there should be little apparent difference in length between skull and foreface. If, however, the foreface is noticeably shorter, it amounts to a fault, the head looking weak and "unfinished." On the other hand, when the eyes are set too high up in the skull and too near the ears, it also amounts to a fault, the head being said to have a "foreign appearance."

The eyes of the Wire Fox Terrier are deep set and should convey intelligence, life, and spirit. The hard, steely, cool look of a Wire can't be avoided. Ch. Sunspryte's Prime Contender, owned by Carol Beattie.

Keen of **expression**. **Eyes** should be dark in color, moderately small, rather deep-set, not prominent, and full of fire, life, and intelligence; as nearly as possible circular in shape, and not too far apart. Anything approaching a yellow eye is most objectionable. **Ears** should be small and V-shaped and of moderate thickness, the flaps neatly folded over and dropping forward close to the checks. The topline of the folded ear should be well above the level of the skull. A pendulous ear, hanging dead by the side of the head like a Hound's, is uncharacteristic of the Terrier, while an ear which is semierect is still more undesirable. **Disqualifications**—Ears prick, tulip or rose.

The topline of the **skull** should be almost flat, sloping slightly and gradually decreasing in width towards the eyes, and should not exceed 3 ½ inches in diameter at the widest part—measuring with the calipers—in the full-grown dog of correct size, the bitch's skull being proportionately narrower. If this measurement is exceeded the skull is termed "coarse," while a full-grown dog with a much narrower skull is termed "bitchy" in head.

Opposite: A Wire Fox Terrier should be "keen of expression", allowing a glimpse into the intelligent, loyal nature of the Wire. Ch. Sunspryte's Prime Contender, owned by Carol Beattie.

The head of the Wire Hair Fox Terrier must be well balanced and in proportion to the rest of the dog.

Although the *foreface* should gradually taper from eye to muzzle and should dip slightly at its juncture with the forehead, it should not "dish" or fall away quickly below the eyes, where it should be full and well made up, but relieved from "wedginess" by a little delicate chiseling. While well-developed *jawbones*, armed with a set of strong, white teeth, impart that appearance of strength to the foreface which is so desirable, an excessive bony or muscular development of the jaws is both unnecessary and unsightly, as it is partly responsible for the full and rounded contour of the cheeks to which the term "cheeky" is applied.

Nose should be black. ***Disqualifications***—Nose white, cherry or spotted to a considerable extent with either of these colors. ***Mouth***—Both upper and lower jaws should be strong and muscular, the **teeth** as nearly as possible level and capable of closing together like a vise—the lower canines locking in front of the upper and the points of the upper incisors slightly overlapping the lower. ***Disqualifications***— Much undershot, or much overshot.

This section allows one to take specific measurements of the head to further define the lean, graceful, but solid working terrier. There are some

The overall appearance of a Wire Fox Terrier when stacked should illustrate all of the breed standard as a whole. Ch. Cheviots Wildwood Alfa Romeo, owned by C. Robin Pensinger.

There are times when the eyes of a Wire Fox Terrier will express love, enjoyment, tenacity, admiration, mischieviousness, as well as a soft, kind, gentle expression.

who say you can't have a head that is too long, however all things must be kept in proportion. The fact that the beard on a Wire Fox Terrier's muzzle can hide a jaw that is overly narrow, weak and short, is something one must be aware of. Should a dog with this type of muzzle be bred to a dog with similar structure, the result can be missing or poor teeth alignment, inability to work, and eventually the inability to chew food. All dog structure has a purpose.

The expression "hard-bitten eye" frequently used by terrier people, while a harsh phrase, mentally conjures the look of perhaps a criminal—or the cold, accusing glare of a police officer who has clocked you at 75 mph in a 55 mph speed zone. The standard may not fully depict the image breeders seek; that is, eyes that are all business, ready, eager, somewhat hyper, darting frequently so as not to miss a single action or non-action, intent and alive, alert, bright, and sparkling, but the expectation is there. One has the sense there is a great deal of activity and motion behind those grinning eyes. A bit more narrowness to the eye, as opposed to a fully circular eye, gives more of the desired mischievous expression. However, the eyes can express fun, love, tenacity, admiration and roguishness, as well as a soft, gentle and kind expression. Just let his family member exhibit an emotion of sadness or trouble, there will be kindness and concern seen in that "hard-bitten" eye, that says "let me fix it for you." While the eyes may be calculating, the heart of a Wire is caring. There are some breeds that put extra emphasis on the head, as well as a demand for a sound animal. The Fox Terrier is not a "head" breed as such, but, it is the head and expression of a Wire that should be considered carefully and is of essential importance when selecting an acceptable specimen.

Without the follow-through of the graceful, arched neck of appropriate length, and the short, level back with a tail that comes straight out of the topline down to a rear that is well angulated and reaches back far enough to allow for leverage and balance in working, sporting and playing; to the straight, perpendicular hocks and tight feet, matched with straight front legs adequately placed under a chest sufficient for lungs and heart to work cohesively— without all of these things one would have something a great deal less than a true Wire Fox Terrier.

A dog's bite is very important to his health. The Wire's teeth should be together as nearly as possible. Ch. Raylu Realistic, owned by Gene S. Bigelow and Judy Franklin.

The proper tail or stern is of utmost importance, it actually predicts the true ability of this animal to function. Ch. Wyrequest's She's All Mine, owned by Mr. and Mrs. Splawn.

Neck, Topline, Body—*Neck* should be clean, muscular, of fair length, free from throatiness and presenting a graceful curve when viewed from the side. The ***back*** should be short and level with no appearance of slackness—the *loins* muscular and very slightly arched. The term "slackness" is applied both to the portion of the back immediately behind the withers when it shows any tendency to dip, and also the flanks when there is too much space between the back ribs and hips, the dog is said to be "short in couplings," "short-coupled," or "well ribbed up." A Terrier can scarcely be too short in back, provided he has sufficient length of neck and liberty of movement. The bitch may be slightly longer in couplings than the dog.

Chest deep and not broad, a too narrow chest being almost as undesirable as a very broad one. Excessive depth of chest and brisket is an impediment to a Terrier when going to ground. The *brisket* should be deep, the front ribs moderately arched, and the back ribs deep and well sprung. Tail should be set on rather high and carried gaily but not curled. It should be of good strength and substance and of fair length—a three-quarters dock is about right—since it affords the only safe grip when handling working Terriers. A very short tail is suitable neither for work nor show.

The proper tail is so vital to a Wire Fox Terrier that once your eye has taken in the outline of the dog as to balance, it should then evaluate the tail. Where the tail comes out of the dog is a strong requirement. It must come right out of the back. A lower tail set generally establishes that the entire rear assembly is a bit more under the dog. The rear extension then is not as dramatic as it could be, and the forward movement will not be as forceful. The tail's thickness should balance with the bone and body mass of the Wire, it should be stiff, and with just a whisper of an angle toward the head. The tail also is a forewarning of the current attitude of the dog. An unattractive tail is one that, with excitement, slams over the back and quivers as it points to the back of the head.

Forequarters—*Shoulders* when viewed from the front should slope steeply downwards from their juncture, with the neck towards the points, which should be fine. When viewed from the side they should be long, well laid back, and should slope obliquely backwards from points to withers, which should always be clean-cut. A shoulder well laid back gives the long forehand which, in combination with a short back, is so desirable in Terrier or Hunter. The elbows should hang perpendicular to the body, working free of the sides, carried straight through in traveling. Viewed from any direction the legs should be straight, the bone of the forelegs strong right down to the feet.

The forequarters of a Wire Fox Terrier must allow the dog a long, easy stride, as well as add greatly to the beauty of the animal.

Wire Fox Terriers are so responsive that they inspire an almost feverish loyalty in their owners.

Feet should be round compact, and not large—the pads tough and well cushioned, and the toes moderately arched and turned neither in nor out. A Terrier with good-shaped forelegs and feet will wear his nails down short by contact with the road surface, the weight of the body being evenly distributed between the toe pads and the heels.

Hindquarters—Should be strong and muscular, quite free from droop or crouch; the thighs long and powerful, the stifles well curved and turned neither in nor out; the hock joints well bent and near the ground; the hocks perfectly upright and parallel with each other when viewed from behind. The worst possible form of hindquarters consists of a short second thigh and a straight stifle, a combination which causes the hind legs to act as props rather than instruments of propulsion. The hind legs should be carried straight through in traveling. Feet as in front.

Coat—The best coats appear to be broken, the hairs having a tendency to twist, and are of dense, wire texture— like coconut matting—the hairs grow-

43

ing so closely and strongly together that, when parted with the fingers, the skin cannot be seen. At the base of these stiff hairs is a shorter growth of finer and softer hair—termed the undercoat. The coat on the sides is never quite so hard as that on the back and quarters. Some of the hardest coats are "crinkly" or slightly waved, but a curly coat is very objectionable. The hair on the upper and lower jaws should be crisp and only sufficiently long to impart an appearance of strength to the foreface. The hair on the forelegs should also be dense and crisp. The coat should average in length from ³/₄ to one inch on shoulders and neck, lengthening to 1 ¹/₂ inches on withers, back, ribs, and quarters. These measurements are given rather as a guide to exhibitors than as an infallible rule, since the length of coat depends on the climate, seasons, and individual animal. The judge must form his own opinion as to what constitutes a "sufficient" coat on the day.

Opposite: The Wire Fox Terrier is a multi-faceted breed, able to be all things to all people, an all-around excellent animal. Ch. Cheviots Lamborghini Diablo, owned by C. Robin Pensinger.

Color—White should predominate; brindle, red, liver or slaty blue are objectionable. Otherwise, color is of little or not importance.

Clothes make the man, so it has been said. The jacket of the Wire Fox Terrier is the essence of this breed. Without a properly prepared wiry, colorful and bright, tight coat, the Fox Terrier loses his character.

White should be the predominant color of the Wire's coat. Markings are of little consequence except if they are ill placed and cause the dog to appear malformed.

Preparation definitely requires dedication and skill, both learned and natural. The employment of illusion, and the groomer whose eye can see the diamond under that unkempt wool, plus the developed techniques of learned shaping, will make for an awesome animal.

White must predominate in this breed, however, where the color is placed on the dog is of little consequence. Except, in the instance of an ill-placed marking that can cause an adverse look to a dog's construction. For example, a spot of color undesirably located high on the withers will make a dog's neck look short, his back will appear long, and will give the appearance of insufficient arch to the neck and will negate the smooth gradual slope into the topline. Again, illusion enters into the picture.

Gait—The movement or action is the crucial test of conformation. The terrier's legs should be carried

Even as a puppy, Ch. Crystcrack Sun Flare, "Devon," owned by Gloria Snellings, shows good confirmation and the easy stride Wire Fox Terriers are known for.

Not until 1876 was a standard written for the Wire Fox Terrier. Before this time dogs were bred by a "flight of fancy" method—different litters resembled different contributing ancestors.

straight forward while traveling, the forelegs hanging perpendicular and swinging parallel to the sides, like the pendulum of a clock. The principal propulsive power is furnished by the hind legs, perfection of action being found in the terrier possessing long thighs and muscular second-thighs well bent at the stifles, which admit of a strong forward thrust or "snatch" of the hocks. When approaching, the fore-legs should form a continuation of the straight of the front, the feet being the same distance apart as the elbows. When stationary it is often difficult to determine whether a dog is slightly out at shoulder but, directly he moves, the defect— if it exists—becomes more apparent, the fore-feet having a tendency to cross, "weave" or "dish." When, on the contrary, the dog is tied at the shoulder, the tendency of the feet is to move wider apart, with a sort of padding action. When the hocks are turned in—cow-hocks—the stifles and feet are turned outwards, resulting in a serious loss of propulsive power. When the hocks are turned outwards the tendency of the hind feet is to cross, resulting in an ungainly waddle.

This Wire Fox Terrier's "Who Me?" expression takes the standard's requirements for temperament to heart!

When looking at a Wire, recognize that the length of the first and second thigh bones are almost equal, the pelvic assembly is lifted very slightly, there is moderate angulation, and you will have that push of hock that ejects the Wire forward. Further, the standard requires short hocks and long thighs. If one selects a dog with a very long thigh and a very short hock, the dog will depict improper balance, will be an incorrect interpretation of the standard, and will be unable to function properly. The hocks must be straight up and down and not wing out, nor be at such an angle so that the toes are under the body but should be straight under the hock.

Temperament— The Terrier should be alert, quick of movement, keen of expression, on the tip-toe of expectation at the slightest provocation.

Disqualifications—Ears prick, tulip or rose. Nose white, cherry or spotted to a considerable extent with either of these colors. Mouth much undershot, or much overshot.

The standard has been clearly explained in a booklet produced by The American Fox Terrier Club, which definitively states what is expected in a Wire. You should contact the American Kennel Club, 51 Madison Avenue, New York, NY 10010 for the address of the current club secretary to obtain this inexpensive booklet.

SELECTING A WIRE FOX TERRIER

What a fun thing! After you have found a breeder you would like to do business with, an opportunity should be made available to you to come and watch the puppies play together. This will be a good way to ascertain temperament, and quality, as well as what puppy has a personality that fits your needs. If you have a young child or children, you certainly don't want the most aggressive puppy in the litter. However, you don't want a puppy that is a shrinking violet and won't defend itself against a baby's innocent but hurtful hands. It is up to you to teach the puppy manners regarding how he lets it be known that he's being hurt.

Watch the puppies—which one plays independently without his littermates? Which one comes right up to you immediately? Is there one that is more willing to stay in your lap, or would he rather be down on the floor playing? After you are satisfied with the temperament of the pups, then look at the structure of the dog. Ask to see the dam and sire, if available. Look

If you should decide to bring a puppy into your life, it is not a decision that should be taken lightly. Owning a puppy is a lot of hard work, there are definite considerations that will have to be discussed.

at the pedigree and see if there are many AKC champions, also look for line breedings in the first three generations. There are three kinds of matings that can be done. Linebreeding is building on one ancestor, but the parents are little, if at all, related to each other through any other ancestors and may involve distant generations. Inbreeding generally

means mating son to mother, father to daughter, brother to sister, or half-brother to half-sister. Family breeding, a term coined by Mr. Lloyd C. Brackett, author of many articles for *Dog World*, and breeder at Long-Worth German Shepherd Kennels, has explained it as the breeding of interrelated animals which does not entirely come under the full auspices of inbreeding or linebreeding. The advantage of line-breeding, a choice made by most conscientious breeders, is predictability in the get. One literally doubles up on the like genes from the parents— be they good or bad.

Now you have selected the square puppy, with the long head, short back, upright tail— only to be told he is "pick of the litter" and must be placed in a "show" home. First, pat yourself on the back for picking a "good one," then re-evaluate your willingness to become involved in the sport of exhibiting purebred dogs. Most breeders will not part with their "pick bitch" for any amount of money. However, you may be able to negotiate an agreement that will allow the breeder to have her cake and eat it too! Be willing to sign a statement agreeing to have the dog shown on a shared expense basis, which includes grooming costs (if you are unwilling to tackle that) and a puppy or puppies back from the first litter. Encourage the

Is your lifestyle, or that of your family ready for a new addition? Will someone have the time and patience it takes to make your puppy into a fulfilled, happy, and well-trained member of your household?

Opposite: A Wire Fox Terrier's breeding is of great importance. Do your homework. Research breeders in your area until you find one that you are comfortable doing business with. A Wire purchased from a reputable breeder will be a wonderful pet— he is smart, clean, loving, and protective.

50

breeder to select the stud, as she knows more history behind her dogs and which stud dogs available would complement her line and your puppy. Remember, there is a fee for using a stud dog, plus there are costs involved with raising a litter of puppies. But the delight, education, and experience your family will share with a litter of puppies is worth all costs.

Should you feel that a show puppy is out of the question for you, then you can re-evaluate the litter with less perfection in mind. If you have selected a

After choosing a breeder, an opportunity to visit the kennel and view a litter should be made available to you. Take careful notice of the things you see there. Are the puppies clean and healthy looking? Do they seem happy and well fed? Are there any sires or dams on the premises? Ch. Raylu's Starquest, owned by Gene S. Bigelow, was retired to pet life and clipped down.

reputable breeder, they will not try to sell you a sickly or unhealthy puppy without your full knowledge.

Contact the American Kennel Club for the name and address of the secretary of the American Fox Terrier Club for a list of breeders in your area. Better yet—find out when there will be a dog show nearby, and what time Fox Terriers are to be shown, and go to several shows to learn as much as you can. Buying a puppy is not like buying a new computer—it is more like adopting a child, and the responsibility of caring for it is strictly up to you.

YOUR PUPPY'S NEW HOME

Before making the trip to pick up your puppy, be sure to purchase the items you will need for his basic care. If you wait until his arrival at home, important things will be forgotten in all the excitement. Welwyre puppies, owned by Harry and Darlene Welsh.

Before actually collecting your puppy, it is better that you purchase the basic items you will need in advance of the pup's arrival date. This allows you more opportunity to shop around and ensure you have exactly what you want rather than having to buy lesser quality in a hurry.

It is always better to collect the puppy as early in the day as possible. In most instances this will mean that the puppy has a few hours with your family before it is time to retire for his first night's sleep away from his former home.

If the breeder is local, then you may not need any form of box to place the puppy in when you bring him home. A member of the family can hold the pup in his lap—duly protected by some towels just in case the puppy becomes car sick! Be sure to advise the breeder at what time you hope to arrive for the puppy, as this will obviously influence the feeding of the pup that morning or afternoon. If you arrive early in the

If the trip home is a long one, be sure to give your puppy ample opportunity to stretch his legs as well as relieve himself.

day, then they will likely only give the pup a light breakfast so as to reduce the risk of travel sickness.

If the trip will be of a few hours duration, you should take a travel crate with you. The crate will provide your pup with a safe place to lie down and rest during the trip. During the trip, the puppy will no doubt wish to relieve his bowels, so you will have to make a few stops. On a long journey you may need a rest yourself, and can take the opportunity to let the puppy get some fresh air. However, do not let the puppy walk where there may have been a lot of other dogs because he might pick up an infection. Also, if he relieves his bowels at such a time, do not just leave the feces where they were dropped. This is the height of irresponsibility. It has resulted in many public parks and other places actually banning dogs. You can purchase poop-scoops from your pet shop and should have them with you whenever you are taking the dog out where he might foul a public place.

Your journey home should be made as quickly as possible. If it is a hot day, be sure the car interior is amply supplied with fresh air. It should never be too hot or too cold for the puppy. The pup must never be placed where he might be subject to a draft. If the journey requires an overnight stop at a motel, be aware that other guests will not appreciate a puppy crying half the night. You must regard the puppy as a baby and comfort him so he does not cry for long periods. The worst thing you can do is to shout at or smack him. This will mean your relationship is off to a really bad start. You wouldn't smack a baby, and your puppy is still very much just this.

ON ARRIVING HOME

By the time you arrive home your puppy will probably be tired and a little confused. Try not to overwhelm him—let him inspect his surroundings without the interference of too many people. Offer him a cool drink and a light meal and your puppy will probably settle in for a much needed nap.

By the time you arrive home the puppy may be very tired, in which case he should be taken to his sleeping area and allowed to rest. Children should not be allowed to interfere with the pup when he is sleeping. If the pup is not tired, he can be allowed to investigate his new home—but always under your close supervision. After a short look around, the puppy will no doubt appreciate a light meal and a drink of water. Do not overfeed him at his first meal because he will be in an excited state and more likely to be sick.

Although it is an obvious temptation, you should not invite friends and neighbors around to see the new arrival until he has had at least 48 hours in which to settle down. Indeed, if you can delay this longer then do so, especially if the puppy is not fully vaccinated. At the very least, the visitors might introduce some local bacteria on their clothing that the puppy is not immune to. This aspect is always a risk when a pup has been moved some distance, so the fewer people the pup meets in the first week or so the better.

DANGERS IN THE HOME

Your home holds many potential dangers for a little mischievous puppy, so you must think about these in advance and be sure he is protected from them. The more obvious are as follows:

Open Fires. All open fires should be protected by a mesh screen guard so there is no danger of the pup being burned by spitting pieces of coal or wood.

Electrical Wires. Puppies just love chewing on things, so be sure that all electrical appliances are neatly hidden from view and are not left plugged in when not in use. It is not sufficient simply to turn the plug switch to the off position—pull the plug from the socket.

Open Doors. A door would seem a pretty innocuous object, yet with a strong draft it could kill or injure a puppy easily if it is slammed shut. Always ensure

Believe it or not your home holds many dangers for a mischievous little puppy. It is often a good idea to "puppy-proof" your home before his arrival. Be aware, many situations can be dangerous to a puppy. Wire Fox Terriers owned by Gail and Mike Obradovich.

there is no risk of this happening. It is most likely during warm weather when you have windows or outside doors open and a sudden gust of wind blows through.

Balconies. If you live in a high-rise building, obviously the pup must be protected from falling. Be sure he cannot get through any railings on your patio, balcony, or deck.

Ponds and Pools. A garden pond or a swimming pool is a very dangerous place for a little puppy to be near. Be sure it is well screened so there is no risk of the pup falling in. It takes barely a minute for a pup—or a child—to drown.

The Kitchen. While many puppies will be kept in the kitchen, at least while they are toddlers and not able to control their bowel movements, this is a room full of danger—especially while you are cooking. When cooking, keep the puppy in a play pen or in another room where he is safely out of harm's way. Alternatively, if you have a carry box or crate, put him in this so he can still see you but is well protected.

A swimming pool can be a very dangerous place for your Wire —it only takes a moment for a puppy to drown. Be sure your Wire Fox Terrier is closely supervised when near any body of water. DunGar puppies, owned by John and Lynn Killeen.

Be aware, when using washing machines, that more than one puppy has clambered in and decided to have a nap and received a wash instead! If you leave the washing machine door open and leave the room for any reason, then be sure to check inside the machine before you close the door and switch on.

Small Children. Toddlers and small children should never be left unsupervised with puppies. In spite of such advice it is amazing just how many people not only do this but also allow children to pull and maul pups. They should be taught from the outset that a puppy is not a plaything to be dragged about the home—and they should be promptly scolded if they disobey.

Children must be shown how to lift a puppy so it is safe. Failure by you to correctly educate your children about dogs could one day result in their getting a very nasty bite or scratch. When a puppy is lifted, his weight must always be supported. To lift the pup, first place your right hand under his chest. Next, secure the pup by using your left hand to hold his neck. Now you can lift him and bring him close to your chest. Never lift a pup by his ears and, while he can be lifted by the scruff of his neck where the fur is loose, there is no reason ever to do this, so don't.

Beyond the dangers already cited you may be able to think of other ones that are specific to your home—steep basement steps or the like. Go around your home and check out all potential problems—you'll be glad you did.

Small children should be closely supervised when interacting with puppies. Both parties need to be taught the appropriate way to interact with one another. Lauren Ashley Harris with Crystcrack Radiant Sun and Ch. Crystcrack Sun Flare, owned by Gloria Snellings.

THE FIRST NIGHT

The first few nights a puppy spends away from his mother and littermates are quite traumatic for him. He will feel very lonely, maybe cold, and will certainly miss the heartbeat of his siblings when sleeping. To help overcome his loneliness it may help to place a clock next to his bed—one with a loud tick. This will in some way soothe him, as the clock ticks to a rhythm not dissimilar from a heart beat. A cuddly toy may also help in the first few weeks. A dim nightlight may provide some comfort to the puppy, because his eyes will not yet be fully able to see in the dark. The puppy may want to leave his bed for a drink or to relieve himself.

The first few nights a puppy spends away from his littermates are sometimes difficult. Suddenly he finds himself all alone. Be sure to offer your puppy special consideration on these first few evenings—he needs you! DunGar puppies, owned by John and Lynn Killeen.

If the pup does whimper in the night, there are two things you should not do. One is to get up and chastise him, because he will not understand why you are shouting at him; and the other is to rush to comfort him every time he cries because he will quickly realize that if he wants you to come running all he needs to do is to holler loud enough!

By all means give your puppy some extra attention on his first night, but after this quickly refrain from so doing. The pup will cry for a while but then settle down and go to sleep. Some pups are, of course, worse than others in this respect, so you must use balanced judgment in the matter. Many owners take their pups to bed with them, and there is certainly nothing wrong with this.

The pup will be no trouble in such cases. However, you should only do this if you intend to let this be a permanent arrangement, otherwise it is hardly fair to the puppy. If you have decided to have two puppies, then they will keep each other company and you will have few problems.

OTHER PETS

If you have other pets in the home then the puppy must be introduced to them under careful supervision. Puppies will get on just fine with any other pets—but you must make due allowance for the respective sizes of the pets concerned, and appreciate that your puppy has a rather playful nature. It would be very foolish to leave him with a young rabbit. The pup will want to play and might bite the bunny and get altogether too rough with it. Kittens are more able to

defend themselves from overly cheeky pups, who will get a quick scratch if they overstep the mark. The adult cat could obviously give the pup a very bad scratch, though generally cats will jump clear of pups and watch them from a suitable vantage point. Eventually they will meet at ground level where the cat will quickly hiss and box a puppy's ears. The pup will soon learn to respect an adult cat; thereafter they will probably develop into great friends as the pup matures into an adult dog.

Most puppies will get along with other animals. Be sure to closely supervise all introductions. Remember that animals will often come to their own understandings much more readily than we would assume. Wire Fox Terrier Bailey owned by Jean Mason.

HOUSETRAINING

Undoubtedly, the first form of training your puppy will undergo is in respect to his toilet habits. To achieve this you can use either newspaper, or a large litter tray filled with soil or lined with newspaper. A puppy cannot control his bowels until he is a few months old, and not fully until he is an adult. Therefore you must anticipate his needs and be prepared for a few accidents. The prime times a pup will urinate and defecate are shortly after he wakes up from a sleep, shortly after he has eaten, and after he has been playing awhile. He will usually whimper and start searching the room for a suitable place. You must quickly pick him up and place him on the newspaper or in the litter tray. Hold him in position gently but firmly. He might jump out of the box without doing anything on the first one or two occasions, but if you simply repeat the procedure every time you think he wants to relieve himself then eventually he will get the message.

When he does defecate as required, give him plenty of praise, telling him what a good puppy he is. The litter tray or newspaper must, of course, be cleaned or replaced after each use—puppies do not like using a dirty toilet any more than you do. The pup's toilet can be placed near the kitchen door and as he gets older the tray can be placed outside while the door is open. The pup will then start to use it while he is outside. From that time on, it is easy to get the pup to use a given area of the yard.

Crate training is an effective way to house break your puppy. A puppy will think of his crate as his den, and no dog will mess in his living area. Be sure to place a few of your puppy's favorite toys inside his crate to keep him occupied.

Many breeders recommend the popular alternative of crate training. Upon bringing the pup home, introduce him to his crate. The open wire crate is the best choice, placed in a restricted, draft-free area of the home. Put the pup's Nylabone® and other favorite toys in the crate along with a wool blanket or other suitable bedding. The puppy's natural cleanliness instincts prohibit him from soiling in the place where he sleeps, his crate. The puppy should be allowed to go in and out of the open crate during the day, but he should sleep in the crate at the night and at other intervals during the day. Whenever the pup is taken out of his crate, he should be brought outside (or to his newspapers) to do his business. Never use the crate as a place of punishment. You will see how quickly your pup takes to his crate, considering it as his own safe haven from the big world around him.

One of the first steps toward making your puppy a welcome member of the family is getting him house trained. It is important to be patient and to keep in mind that your puppy wants to learn what you have to teach him! Wire Fox Terrier puppy owned by Virginia and Raymond Splawn.

THE EARLY DAYS

You will no doubt be given much advice on how to bring up your puppy. This will come from dog-owning friends, neighbors, and through articles and books you may read on the subject. Some of the advice will be sound, some will be nothing short of rubbish. What you should do above all else is to keep an open mind and let common sense prevail over prejudice and worn-out ideas that have been handed down over the centuries. There is no one way that is superior to all others, no more than there is no one dog that is exactly a replica of another.

Be sure to provide your puppy with some form of identification shortly after he arrives home. In the event that a puppy is lost, tags, tattooing, or microchipping will all be of great assistance in locating him. Wire Fox Terrier owned by Raymond and Virginia Splawn.

Each is an individual and must always be regarded as such.

A dog never becomes disobedient, unruly, or a menace to society without the full consent of his owner. Your puppy may have many limitations, but the singular biggest limitation he is confronted with in so many instances is his owner's inability to understand his needs and how to cope with them.

IDENTIFICATION

It is a sad reflection on our society that the number of dogs and cats stolen every year runs into many thousands. To these can be added the number that get lost. If you do not want your cherished pet to be lost or stolen, then you should see that he is carrying a permanent identification number, as well as a temporary tag on his collar.

Permanent markings come in the form of tattoos placed either inside the pup's ear flap, or on the inner side of a pup's upper rear leg. The number given is then recorded with one of the national registration companies. Research laboratories will not purchase dogs carrying numbers as they realize these are clearly someone's pet, and not abandoned animals. As a result, thieves will normally abandon dogs so marked and this at least gives the dog a chance to be taken to the police or the dog pound, when the number can be traced and the dog reunited with its family. The only problem with this method at this time is that there are a number of registration bodies, so it is not always apparent which one the dog is registered with (as you provide the actual number). However, each registration body is aware of his competitors and will normally be happy to supply their addresses. Those holding the dog can check out which one you are with. It is not a perfect system, but until such is developed it's the best available.

Another permanent form of identification is the microchip, a computer chip that is no bigger than a grain of rice, that is injected between the dog's shoulder blades. The dog feels no discomfort. The dog also recieves a tag that says he is microchipped. If the dog is lost and picked up by the humane society, they can trace the owner by scanning the microchip. It is the safest form of identification.

A temporary tag takes the form of a metal or plastic disk large enough for you to place the dog's name and your phone number on it—maybe even your address as well. In virtually all places you will be required to obtain a license for your puppy. This may not become applicable until the pup is six months old, but it might apply regardless of his age. Much depends upon the state within a country, or the country itself, so check with your veterinarian if the breeder has not already advised you on this.

Always provide your Wire Fox Terrier with a collar and tags, it is the simplest form of identification, and a good first step in keeping your dog out of harm's way. Dungar kennel Wire Fox Terriers owned by John and Lyn Killeen.

GROOMING A WIRE FOX TERRIER

The grooming of a pet Wire Fox Terrier need not be as involved as that of the show dog. Your dog's health should take precedence over all else.

Of the 141 American Kennel Club recognized breeds, grooming a Wire Fox Terrier is a unique method of presentation. But within the specific terrier group it is the norm. There are two methods of grooming a Wire Fox Terrier, one being highly preferential over the other. The choices are either stripping or clipping the coat. Stripping a Wire coat definitely requires talent. To achieve the bright color intended on the Wire coat, it must be stripped. If clippers are used on the coat, it becomes a dull, washed-out gray, soft color and is most unappealing. However, sometimes this less desirable method is the better choice due to time, family obligations, and pocketbook. Love and respect of one's family pet should not be affected by what the dog wears! Health care takes precedence over all else.

THE SHOW TRIM

Should you decide to have that special relationship with your dog by learning the art of grooming him yourself, here are some techniques.

The Wire Fox Terrier has a double coat. It is composed of a stiff, wiry outer coat with brilliant color and frosty, alive white hairs, along with the soft, downy, nondescript, gray color of the undercoat. All must be available to present the picture of embellished elegance that embodies the Wire Fox Terrier.

Stripping, plucking, and grooming are words that are synonymous and are explained as the art of hand removing hair from the body, head and neck of a Wire to allow for growth of a new coat. There is a warranted reason for doing this. The cold, damp climate of the English hunt required a dog that was weatherproof. Also, if this procedure is not performed, the wiry hair, as it grows in length, loses its bright hues, looks gray in color and feels soft in texture. It becomes loose, dies at the root, and eventually falls out hair by hair, but not before it is a good three to four inches long— very unsightly. In order to maintain the close contoured jacket required for a Wire Fox Terrier, this lengthy dead hair must be pulled out by hand, and removal of the fluffy undercoat is done at the same time.

The procedure for grooming a Wire Fox Terrier for show is fairly involved—it is known as stripping.

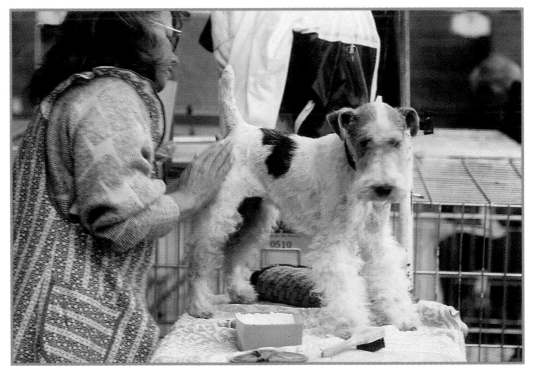

A well groomed Wire Fox Terrier is a sight to behold.

Timing for stripping the Wire coat is critical to the schedule of dog shows entered. Depending on how fast an individual dog's coat grows back determines how early stripping begins. A general rule of thumb could be about eight to twelve weeks prior to the show for the first stripping and four to six weeks for the remainder steps. To explain: Certain areas of the dog must be kept short, i.e.; the throat and chest, sides of the neck, head and ears, and back of tail. The areas that require a bit more length are the crown of the neck and the body, with the front of the tail being somewhat in between. The legs and beard are never stripped clean, but allowed to grow to a maximum length with periodic removal of dead hairs to keep the furnishings vibrant and wiry, and to shape the look of the legs.

Taking a stripping knife in hand, (a semi-dull flat, short bladed instrument with a handle), start at the top of the neck in an approximate two inch path, place a manageable amount of hair between thumb and knife blade, moving your hand and arm straight down in the direction that the hair grows, literally pull/snatch the hair out. It is not a jerking motion, but more of a quick pull with determination. With the hair being dead, this action does not hurt the dog. There are however, certain sensitive areas that need to be stripped with compassion, speed and efficiency. If the root of the hair blade is not removed, and the shaft is broken off as if it were cut, the coat will not grow back from new growth, but will continue growing from the same old hair blade.

With the strip of outer wire coat removed from the length of the neck, continue this method down the spine to the tail and over the ribs down to the lower edge of the body to the skirt left on the underside of the ribcage and underchest. Accentuating the tuckup gives the Wire a natural waist. When this time-consuming but rewarding task has been completed, the dog will then be left with a soft, fuzzy somewhat oily feeling undercoat in the stripped area of future mane

on the neck ridge and body. There will be great lengths of hair on the head, ears, forechest, and sides of neck, and the stripper's hand and arm will be quite tough and strong. Removal of the cottony undergrowth from the stripped area can be delayed for a couple of weeks so that it will come back into visible growth at a later date than the outer hair. A working terrier may need this protective woolly undershirt, but it negates the tight, flat flashy jacket for the show dog and should be removed continuously as best as possible. However, a jacket without any undercoat becomes an open, loose-fitting coat. A little is necessary, but a lot ruins the picture.

The next step, a few weeks later, is to strip the sides of the neck, throat, chest, back of tail, and finally the

You can groom your pet Wire just about anywhere—after a romp in the park it might be just the thing to do while he's resting.

Getting your Wire used to grooming at an early age is recommended. It will be easier for all concerned if your Wire knows what to expect. You never know, he may grow to enjoy the attention!

head and ears. A factor that enters into the picture at this point that can pose a problem is during the time when the ears have all hair removed, the lack of weight may cause the flap or leather to lift higher than is acceptable. Using a removable glue, you may carefully affix the ear to the skull or attach a minor weight to the inside of the flap near the point of the ear. There are a number of easily removable glues that will hold a non-invasive object, or the glue itself may be enough. However, removing the object from the ear must be done in time prior to the show for the ear to go back to its natural arch, which by show date should have a covering of hair to weigh it down again and re-seat itself in a proper fold. This method is frequently used while the puppy is teething, which causes the ears to lift and do strange things! It is the same principal for placing weights on show horse's ankles during training. This forces the horse to exert more effort in lifting his feet, so that when the weights are removed the mind is set to lift the foot rather vigorously, thus giving the picture of a beautiful high-stepping prancing horse. Merely a trick of the trade!

Undercoat on the head, cheeks and ears will mar the finished look. Careful picking of these areas is important. At the time the second phase of stripping is being done, shaping of the legs and underchest should begin. Leaving longer furnishings at the top of the legs where the stripped body coat meets the unstripped leg gives a Wire an elbows-out look or a western chaps appearance. Blending these areas is vastly important for the movement of the dog. The final stripped body coat length must be mentally visualized while shaping the legs.

Blending the beard into the cheeks requires a delicate, artistic eye. Leave the eyebrows longer, separated in the middle, and longer over the inside corner of the eye than the outer corner with a tapering effect. The beard is profuse, flat not blowing, and covers the upper muzzle, whereas the lower jaw furnishings are quite long and cover more of a goatee area.

No grooming line is abrupt, but is a blending, smoothing, and gradually flowing visual look. This is where the real talent and expertise enters the picture. When groomed to completion, the less contrived the Wire Fox Terrier looks, the more natural his appearance will be and the greater his chances of winning.

A Wire Fox Terrier beautifully conditioned in prime coat length is always a total pleasure to look at and an impressive specimen of the animal kingdom.

Peter Green, along with his son, Andrew, who are handlers from Pennsylvania, have an impressive talent for presentation that results in many wins in the show ring. Peter, who got his training in his native Wales, tells us: "There is a method of maintaining a Wire Fox Terrier's coat that allows extended exhibiting time on the same coat, and that is called "rolling" the coat. It goes without saying that the amount of time one is able to "roll" the coat depends entirely on the quality of hair the dog grows.

"Keeping a Wire Fox Terrier in coat starts soon after you strip the dog out. Approximately two weeks after the initial stripping one goes over the body again removing any long undercoat which has grown. Use a fine dull knife or preferably your fingers. The other necessary tool is a hound glove with soft, short bristles to be sure not to bruise the skin. This is also a good time to give a medicated bath. Brush and comb furnishings and remove long, straggly hairs and give the legs a short but round look.

"After another two weeks I start on the dog's body coat in earnest—which really means that it should be hound gloved with the same glove. By now the new coat should be starting through the skin. The flat work and furnishings should only be trimmed once a week, but hound glove brushing should be a daily event.

"By the eighth to tenth week your dog should now be ready for show, and you hopefully have a lovely new coat of excellent color and texture—a crisp hard outer coat with a soft undercoat. Now it is up to you to brush this coat and hound glove as often as possible to keep the coat.

"If you take down the flat work early and on the same day, i.e., each Monday; that should keep it growing nice and even so it will always look good on show days. The hound glove you now have can be wire on one side and thick horse hair on the other, or separate hound gloves, whichever you are able to buy.

"Your eye has, we hope, helped you put the correct outline on your dog leaving the hair a little longer in parts and a bit shorter in others. The secret is now to keep this coat as tight as possible. The more you work the better the result.

"I like to use the horsehair glove or brush the coat every day for about ten minutes. Then either with your fingers or a dull knife go all over the dog's body picking off any hairs that stand away from the body. This

Doing time on the grooming table! Grooming does not have to be an unpleasurable experience—some dogs find it relaxing and it may afford you some much needed quiet time with your Wire.

Proper grooming is imperative if you plan for your Wire Fox Terrier to have a career in the show ring. The Wire cannot be properly presented without the correct style of coat. Ch. Cheviots Chitty Bang Bang, owned by C. Robin Pensinger.

should be done daily, if possible, or at least every few days.

"When preparing for the show and a final trim, I lightly rake the coat with a medium rake, using a fine rake where the hips and top of hind legs meet, to get out any excessive undercoat, follow with the wire hound glove and finish up with a nice medium hair brush to keep it looking good. The idea is to keep the top coat short and flat with just enough undercoat to give the coat density.

"Each time you take a little dead, dry hair out, some new hair will start to grow in its place, and keep the coat growing. It doesn't hurt to bathe the coat about once a month, too, but you have to make sure to dry the coat and towel it until every hair is lying properly flat in the correct position. It's no good putting the dog away damp as the hair will soon explode in all directions.

"Rolling the coat on a Wire Fox Terrier is not difficult especially if you have a good hard coat to work with. It just takes dedication, and about half an hour a day. Brush and Shape! Pick a few hairs here, and a few there, always looking for the dry dead hairs that are spoiling the nice tight coat."

FEEDING YOUR WIRE FOX TERRIER

Today there are literally hundreds of prepared foods on the market for your dog, and many are specially formulated for puppies. Be sure to ask your breeder for some general guidelines as to what and how much your pup should be eating.

Dog owners today are fortunate in that they live in an age when considerable cash has been invested in the study of canine nutritional requirements. This means dog food manufacturers are very concerned about ensuring that their foods are of the best quality. The result of all of their studies, apart from the food itself, is that dog owners are bombarded with advertisements telling them why they must purchase a given brand. The number of products available to you is unlimited, so it is hardly surprising to find that dogs in general suffer from obesity and an excess of vitamins, rather than the reverse. Be sure to feed age-appropriate food—puppy food up to one year of age, adult food thereafter. Generally breeders recommend dry food supplemented by canned, if needed.

Be sure that cool, fresh water is made available to your Wire Fox Terrier at all times.

FACTORS AFFECTING NUTRITIONAL NEEDS

Activity Level. A dog that lives in a country environment and is able to exercise for long periods of the day will need more food than the same breed of dog living in an apartment and given little exercise.

Quality of the Food. Obviously the quality of food will affect the quantity required by a puppy. If the nutritional content of a food is low then the puppy will need more of it than if a better quality food was fed.

Balance of Nutrients and Vitamins. Feeding a puppy the correct balance of nutrients is not easy because the average person is not able to measure out ratios of one to another, so it is a case of trying to see that nothing is in excess. However, only tests, or your veterinarian, can be the source of reliable advice.

Genetic and Biological Variation. Apart from all of the other considerations, it should be remembered that each puppy is an individual. His genetic make-up will influence not only his physical characteristics but also his metabolic efficiency. This being so, two pups from the same litter can vary quite a bit in the amount of food they need to perform the same function under the same conditions. If you consider the potential combinations of all of these factors then you will see that pups of a given breed could vary quite a bit in the amount of food they will need. Before discussing feeding quantities it is valuable to know at least a little about the composition of food and its role in the body.

COMPOSITION AND ROLE OF FOOD

The main ingredients of food are protein, fats, and carbohydrates, each of which is needed in relatively large quantities when compared to the other needs of vitamins and minerals. The other vital ingredient of food is, of course, water. Although all foods obviously contain some of the basic ingredients needed for an animal to survive, they do not all contain the ingredients in the needed ratios or type. For example, there are many forms of protein, just as there are many types of carbohydrates. Both of these compounds are found in meat and in vegetable matter—but not all of those that are needed will be in one particular meat or vegetable. Plants, especially, do not contain certain amino acids that are required for the synthesis of certain proteins needed by dogs.

Likewise, vitamins are found in meats and vegetable matter, but vegetables are a richer source of most. Meat contains very little carbohydrates. Some vitamins can be synthesized by the dog, so do not need to be supplied via the food. Dogs are carnivores and this means their digestive tract has evolved to need a high quantity of meat as com-

Carrots are rich in fiber, carbohydrates and vitamin A. The Carrot Bone™ from Nylabone® is a durable chew containing no plastics or artificial ingredients of any kind. It can be served as-is, in a bone-hard form, or microwaved to a biscuity consistency—

pared to humans. The digestive system of carnivores is unable to break down the tough cellulose walls of plant matter, but it is easily able to assimilate proteins from meat.

In order to gain its needed vegetable matter in a form that it can cope with, the carnivore eats all of its prey. This includes the partly digested food within the stomach. In commercially prepared foods, the cellulose is broken down by cooking. During this process the vitamin content is either greatly reduced or lost altogether. The manufacturer therefore adds vitamins once the heat process has been completed. This is why commercial foods are so useful as part of a feeding regimen, providing they are of good quality and from a company that has prepared the foods very carefully.

To combat boredom and relieve your Wire Hair's natural desire to chew, there's nothing better than a Roar-Hide™. Unlike common rawhide, this bone won't turn into a gooey mess when chewed on, so your dog won't choke on small pieces of it, and your carpet won't be stained by it. The Roar-Hide™ is completely edible and is high in protein (over 86%) and low in fat (less than 1/3 of 1%). The Roar-Hide™ is just right for your Wire Hair.

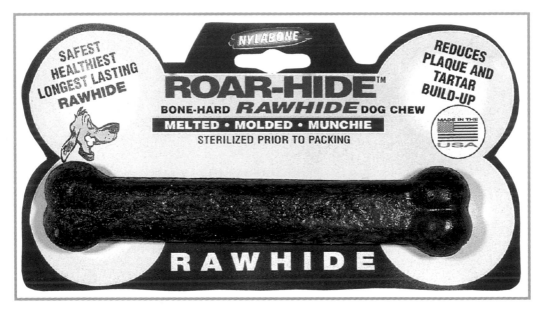

Proteins

These are made from amino acids, of which at least ten are essential if a puppy is to maintain healthy growth. Proteins provide the building blocks for the puppy's body. The richest sources are meat, fish and poultry, together with their by-products. The latter will include milk, cheese, yogurt, fishmeal, and eggs. Vegetable matter that has a high protein content includes soy beans, together with numerous corn and other plant extracts that have been dehydrated. The actual protein content needed in the diet will be determined both by the activity level of the dog and his age. The total protein need will also be influenced by the digestibility factor of the food given.

Fats

These serve numerous roles in the puppy's body. They provide insulation against the cold, and help buffer the organs from knocks and general activity shocks. They provide the richest source of energy, and reserves of this, and they are vital in the transport of vitamins and other nutrients, via the blood, to all other organs. Finally, it is the fat content within a diet that gives it palatability. It is important that the fat content of a diet should not be excessive. This is because the high energy content of fats (more than twice that of protein or carbohydrate) will increase the overall energy content of the diet. The puppy will adjust its food intake to that of its energy needs, which are obviously more easily met in a high-energy diet. This will mean that while the fats are providing the energy needs of the puppy, the over-all diet may not be providing its protein, vitamin, and mineral needs, so signs of protein deficiency will become apparent. Rich sources of fats are meat, their byproducts (butter, milk), and vegetable oils, such as safflower, olive, corn or soy bean.

Your Wire will be happier and his teeth and gums healthier if you give him a POPpup™ to chew on. Every POPpup™ is 100% edible and enhanced with dog friendly ingredients like liver, cheese, spinach, chicken, carrots, or potatoes. What you won't find in a POPpup™ is salt, sugar, alcohol, plastic, or preservatives. You can even microwave a POPpup™ to turn it into a huge crackly treat for your Wire to enjoy.

Carbohydrates

These are the principal energy compounds given to puppies and adult dogs. Their inclusion within most commercial brand dog foods is for cost, rather than dietary needs. These compounds are more commonly

known as sugars, and they are seen in simple or complex compounds of carbon, hydrogen, and oxygen. One of the simple sugars is called glucose, and it is vital to many metabolic processes. When large chains of glucose are created, they form compound sugars. One of these is called glycogen, and it is found in the cells of animals. Another, called starch, is the material that is found in the cells of plants.

Vitamins

These are not foods as such but chemical compounds that assist in all aspects of an animal's life. They help in so many ways that to attempt to describe these effectively would require a chapter in itself. Fruits are a rich source of vitamins, as is the liver of most animals. Many vitamins are unstable and easily destroyed by light, heat, moisture, or rancidity. An excess of vitamins, especially A and D, has been proven to be very harmful. Provided a puppy is receiving a balanced diet, it is most unlikely there will be a deficiency, whereas hypervitaminosis (an excess of vitamins) has become quite common due to owners and breeders feeding unneeded supplements. The only time you should feed extra vitamins to your puppy is if your veterinarian advises you to.

Minerals

These provide strength to bone and cell tissue, as well as assist in many metabolic processes. Examples are calcium, phosphorous, copper, iron, magnesium, selenium, potassium, zinc, and sodium. The recommended amounts of all minerals in the diet has not been fully established. Calcium and phosphorous are known to be important, especially to puppies. They help in forming strong bone. As with vitamins, a mineral deficiency is most unlikely in pups given a good and varied diet. Again, an excess can create problems—this applying equally to calcium.

Water

This is the most important of all nutrients, as is easily shown by the fact that the adult dog is made up of about 60 percent water, the puppy containing an even higher percentage. Dogs must retain a water balance, which means that the total intake should be balanced by the total output. The intake comes either by direct input (the tap or its equiva-

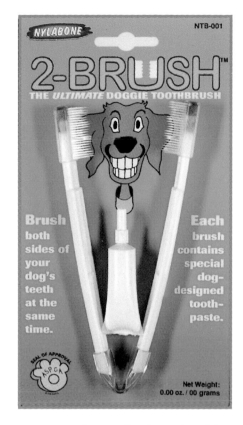

2-Brush™ by Nylabone® is made with two toothbrushes to clean both sides of your dog's teeth at the same time. Each brush contains a reservoir designed to apply the toothpaste, which is specially formulated for dogs, directly into the toothbrush.

lent), plus water released when food is oxidized, known as metabolic water (remember that all foods contain the elements hydrogen and oxygen that recombine in the body to create water). A dog without adequate water will lose condition more rapidly than one depleted of food, a fact common to most animal species.

AMOUNT TO FEED

The best way to determine dietary requirements is by observing the puppy's general health and physical appearance. If he is well covered with flesh, shows good bone development and muscle, and is an active alert puppy, then his diet is fine. A puppy will consume about twice as much as an adult (of the same breed). You should ask the breeder of your puppy to show you the amounts fed to their pups and this will be a good starting point.

The puppy should eat his meal in about five to seven minutes. Any leftover food can be discarded or placed into the refrigerator until the next meal (but be sure it is thawed fully if your fridge is very cold).

If the puppy quickly devours its meal and is clearly still hungry, then you are not giving him enough food. If he eats readily but then begins to pick at it, or walks away leaving a quantity, then you are probably giving him too much food. Adjust this at the next meal and you will quickly begin to appreciate what the correct amount is. If, over a number of weeks, the pup starts to look fat, then he is obviously overeating; the reverse is true if he starts to look thin compared with others of the same breed.

Activity level is one of the determining factors when deciding what type of food to offer your dog. There are different formulations now available to correspond to a dog's many needs.

WHEN TO FEED

It really does not matter what times of the day the puppy is fed, as long as he receives the needed quantity of food. Puppies from 8 weeks to 12 or 16 weeks need 3 or 4 meals a day. Older puppies and adult dogs should be fed twice a day. What is most important is that the feeding times are reasonably regular. They can be tailored to fit in with your own timetable—for example, 7 a.m. and 6 p.m. The dog will then expect his meals at these times each day. Keeping regular feeding times and feeding set amounts will help you monitor your puppy's or dog's health. If a dog that's normally enthusiastic about mealtimes and eats readily suddenly shows a lack of interest in food, you'll know something's not right.

TRAINING YOUR WIRE FOX TERRIER

Once your puppy has settled into his new home and responds to his name you can begin his training.

Once your puppy has settled into your home and responds to his name, then you can begin his basic training. Before giving advice on how you should go about doing this, two important points should be made. You should train the puppy in isolation of any potential distractions, and you should keep all lessons very short. It is essential that you have the full attention of your puppy. This is not possible if there are other people about, or televisions and radios on, or other pets in the vicinity. Even when the pup has become a young adult, the maximum time you should allocate to a lesson is about 20 minutes. However, you can give the puppy more than one lesson a day, three being as many as are recommended, each well spaced apart.

Before beginning a lesson, always play a little game with the puppy so he is in an active state of mind and thus more receptive to the matter at hand. Likewise, always end a lesson with fun-time for the pup, and always—this is most important—end on a high note, praising the puppy. Let the lesson end when the pup has done as you require so he receives lots of fuss. This will really build his confidence.

COLLAR AND LEASH TRAINING

Training a puppy to his collar and leash is very easy. Place a collar on the puppy and, although he will initially try to bite at it, he will soon forget it, the more so if you play with him. You can leave the collar on for a few hours. Some people leave their dogs' collars on all of the time, others only when they are taking the dog out. If it is to be left on, purchase a narrow or round one so it does not mark the fur.

Once the puppy ignores his collar, then you can attach the leash to it and let the puppy pull this along behind it for a few minutes. However, if the pup starts to chew at the leash, simply hold the leash but keep it slack and let the pup go where he wants. The idea is to let him get the feel of the leash, but not get in the habit of chewing it. Repeat this a couple of times a day for two days and the pup will get used to the leash without thinking that it will restrain him—which you will not have attempted to do yet.

Next, you can let the pup understand that the leash will restrict his movements. The first time he realizes this, he will pull and buck or just sit down. Immediately call the pup to you and give him lots of fuss. Never tug on the leash so the puppy is dragged along the floor, as this simply implants a negative thought in his mind.

THE COME COMMAND

Come is the most vital of all commands and especially so for the independently minded dog. To teach the puppy to come, let him reach the end of a long lead, then give the command and his name, gently pulling him toward you at the same time. As soon as he associates the word come with the action of moving toward you, pull only when he does not respond immediately. As he starts to come, move back to make him learn that he must come from a distance as well as when he is close to you. Soon you may be able to practice without a leash, but if he is

Come is one of the most important commands, and is essential to all other lessons. It can be taught verbally or with hand signals. Ch. Killwinning Lady Maeve, owned by John and Lynn Killeen.

slow to come or notably disobedient, go to him and pull him toward you, repeating the command. Never scold a dog during this exercise—or any other exercise. Remember the trick is that the puppy must want to come to you. For the very independent dog, hand signals may work better than verbal commands.

THE SIT COMMAND

As with most basic commands, your puppy will learn this one in just a few lessons. You can give the puppy two lessons a day on the sit command but he will make just as much progress with one 15-minute lesson each day. Some trainers will advise you that you should not proceed to other commands until the previous one has been learned really well. However, a bright young pup is quite capable of handling more than one command per lesson, and certainly per day. Indeed, as time progresses, you will be going through each command as a matter of routine before a new one is attempted. This is so the puppy always starts, as well as ends, a lesson on a high note, having successfully completed something.

Call the puppy to you and fuss over him. Place one hand on his hindquarters and the other under his upper chest. Say "Sit" in a pleasant (never harsh) voice. At the same time, push down his rear end and push up under his chest. Now lavish praise on the puppy. Repeat this a few times and your pet will get

Training will help you to put an end to mischief like this. A well trained Wire Fox Terrier will respond quickly to your commands. Wire Fox Terrier owned by Gail and Mike Obradovich.

the idea. Once the puppy is in the sit position you will release your hands. At first he will tend to get up, so immediately repeat the exercise. The lesson will end when the pup is in the sit position. When the puppy understands the command, and does it right away, you can slowly move backwards so that you are a few feet away from him. If he attempts to come to you, simply place him back in the original position and start again. Do not attempt to keep the pup in the sit position for too long. At this age, even a few seconds is a long while and you do not want him to get bored with lessons before he has even begun them.

THE HEEL COMMAND

All dogs should be able to walk nicely on a leash without their owners being involved in a tug-of-war. The heel command will follow leash training. Heel training is best done where you have a wall to one side of you. This will restrict the puppy's lateral movements, so you only have to contend with forward and backward situations. A fence is an alternative, or you can do the lesson in the garage. Again, it is better to do the lesson in private, not on a public sidewalk where there will be many distractions.

With a puppy, there will be no need to use a choke collar as you can be just as effective with a regular one. The leash should be of good length, certainly not too short. You can adjust the space between you, the puppy, and the wall so your pet has only a small amount of room to move sideways. This being so, he will either hang back or pull ahead—the latter is the more desirable state as it indicates a bold pup who is not frightened of you.

Hold the leash in your right hand and pass it through your left. As the puppy moves ahead and strains on the leash, give the leash a quick jerk backwards with your left hand, at the same time saying "Heel." The position you want the pup to be in is such that his chest is level with, or just behind, an imaginary line from your knee. When the puppy is in this position, praise him and begin walking again, and the whole exercise will be repeated. Once the puppy begins to get the message, you can use your left hand to pat the side of your knee so the pup is encouraged to keep close to your side.

It is useful to suddenly do an about-turn when the pup understands the basics. The puppy will now be behind you, so you can pat your knee and say "Heel." As soon as the pup is in the correct position, give him lots of praise. The puppy will now be beginning to associate certain words with certain actions. Whenever he is not in the heel position he will experience displeasure as you jerk the leash, but when he comes alongside you he will receive praise. Given these two options, he will always prefer the latter—assuming he has no other reason to fear you, which would then create a dilemma in his mind.

Once the lesson has been well learned, then you can adjust your pace from a slow walk to a quick one and the puppy will come to adjust. The slow walk is always the more difficult for most puppies, as they are usually anxious to be on the move.

If you have no wall to walk against then things will be a little more difficult because the pup will tend to wander to his left. This means you need to give lateral jerks as well as bring the pup to your side. End the lesson when the pup is walking nicely beside you. Begin the lesson with a few sit commands (which he understands by now), so you're starting with success and praise. If your puppy is nervous on the leash, you should never drag him to your side as you may see so many other people do (who obviously didn't invest in a good book like you did!). If the pup sits down, call him to your side and give lots of praise. The pup must always come to you because he wants to. If he is dragged to your side he will see you doing the dragging—a big negative. When he races ahead he does not see you jerk the leash, so all he knows is that something restricted his movement and, once he was in a given position, you gave him lots of praise. This is using canine psychology to your advantage.

Always try to remember that if a dog must be disciplined, then try not to let him associate the discipline with you. This is not possible in all matters but, where it is, this is definitely to be preferred.

THE STAY COMMAND

This command follows from the sit. Face the puppy and say "Sit." Now step backwards, and as you do, say "Stay." Let the pup remain in the position for only a few seconds before calling him to you and giving lots of praise. Repeat this, but step further back. You do not need to shout at the puppy. Your pet is not deaf; in fact, his hearing is far better than yours. Speak just loudly enough for the pup to hear, yet use a firm voice.

Once your Wire has mastered the sit command you can begin taking lovely pictures like this one. The fact is, training will make your dog happy, and his life more fulfilling. A well-trained dog will be able to accompany you almost anywhere and participate in all aspects of your life. Ch. Bowyre Treette-Fruite, Ch. Welwyre's Mister T, and Ch. Welwyre's Truehart, owned by Harry and Darlene Welsh.

It is obvious that this Wire Hair Fox Terrier is well "trained." Ch. Crystcrack Obsession ROM, owned by Gloria and Kim Snelling.

You can stretch the word to form a "sta-a-a-y." If the pup gets up and comes to you simply lift him up, place him back in the original position, and start again. As the pup comes to understand the command, you can move further and further back.

The next test is to walk away after placing the pup. This will mean your back is to him, which will tempt him to follow you. Keep an eye over your shoulder, and the minute the pup starts to move, spin around and, using a sterner voice, say either "Sit" or "Stay." If the pup has gotten quite close to you, then, again, return him to the original position.

As the weeks go by you can increase the length of time the pup is left in the stay position—but two to three minutes is quite long enough for a puppy. If your puppy drops into a lying position and is clearly more comfortable, there is nothing wrong with this. Likewise, your pup will want to face the direction in which you walked off. Some trainers will insist that the dog faces the direction he was placed in, regardless of whether you move off on his blind side. I have never believed in this sort of obedience because it has no practical benefit.

THE DOWN COMMAND

From the puppy's viewpoint, the down command can be one of the more difficult ones to accept. This is because the position is one taken up by a submissive dog in a wild pack situation. A timid dog will roll over—a natural gesture of submission. A bolder pup will want to get up, and might back off, not feeling he should have to submit to this command. He will feel that he is under attack from you and about to be punished—which is what would be the position in his natural environment. Once he comes to understand this is not the case, he will accept this unnatural position without any problem.

You may notice that some dogs will sit very quickly, but will respond to the down command more slowly—it is their way of saying that they will obey the command, but under protest!

There are two ways to teach this command. One is, in my mind, more intimidating than the other, but it is up to you to decide which one works best for you. The first method is to stand in front of your puppy and bring him to the sit position, with his collar and leash on. Pass the leash under your left foot so that when you

The down command can be the most difficult for a puppy to accept. In the wild the down command represents the position of a submissive dog, as soon as he realizes this isn't the case, your pup should have no further problems.

The stay command will allow you to leave your puppy's side knowing that he will stay where you put him. At first you will only be several feet from your pup, but as training continues you will be able to increase distance and sometimes move out of your puppy's sight entirely. Wire Fox Terriers owned by Jean Mason.

pull on it, the result is that the pup's neck is forced downwards. With your free left hand, push the pup's shoulders down while at the same time saying "Down." This is when a bold pup will instantly try to back off and wriggle in full protest. Hold the pup firmly by the shoulders so he stays in the position for a second or two, then tell him what a good dog he is and give him lots of praise. Repeat this only a few times in a lesson because otherwise the puppy will get bored and upset over this command. End with an easy command that brings back the pup's confidence.

The second method, and the one I prefer, is done as follows: Stand in front of the pup and then tell him to sit. Now kneel down, which is immediately far less intimidating to the puppy than to have you towering above him. Take each of his front legs and pull them forward, at the same time saying "Down." Release the legs and quickly apply light pressure on the shoulders with your left hand. Then, as quickly, say "Good boy" and give lots of fuss. Repeat two or three times only. The pup will learn over a few lessons. Remember, this is a very submissive act on the pup's behalf, so there is no need to rush matters.

RECALL TO HEEL COMMAND

When your puppy is coming to the heel position from an off-leash situation—such as if he has been running free—he should do this in the correct manner. He should pass behind you and take up his position and then sit. To teach this command, have the pup in front of you in the sit position with his collar and leash on. Hold the leash in your right hand. Give him the command to heel, and pat your left knee. As the pup starts to move forward, use your right hand to guide him behind you. If need be you can hold his collar and walk the dog around the back of you to the desired position. You will need to repeat this a few times until the dog understands what is wanted.

When he has done this a number of times, you can try it without the collar and leash. If the pup comes up toward your left side, then bring him to the sit position in front of you, hold his collar and walk him around the back of you. He will eventually understand and automatically pass around your back each time. If the dog is already behind you when you recall him, then he should automatically come to your left side, which you will be patting with your hand.

When your puppy is coming to the heel position from an off leash situation he must pass behind you, take up his position and then sit. The recall to heel command is very helpful when training a dog for the field or just letting him have a run in the park.

Opposite: Training will open up many possibilities to your Wire Fox Terrier, a well trained dog has the world at his feet! Halcar Desert Shield NAC, NA, JE, CGCI, TDI, owned by C. Wanwright.

THE NO COMMAND

This is a command that must be obeyed every time without fail. There are no halfway stages, he must be 100-percent reliable. Most delinquent dogs have never been taught this command; included in these are the jumpers, the barkers, and the biters. Were your puppy to approach a poisonous snake or any other potential danger, the no command, coupled with the recall, could save his life. You do not need to give a specific lesson for this command because it will crop up time and again in day-to-day life.

If the puppy is chewing a slipper, you should approach the pup, take hold of the slipper, and say "No" in a stern voice. If he jumps onto the furniture, lift him off and say "No" and place him gently on the floor. You must be consistent in the use of the command and apply it every time he is doing something you do not want him to do.

Puppy play can often lead to mischief. While socialization and play are essential, such activities should not become destructive or unruly.

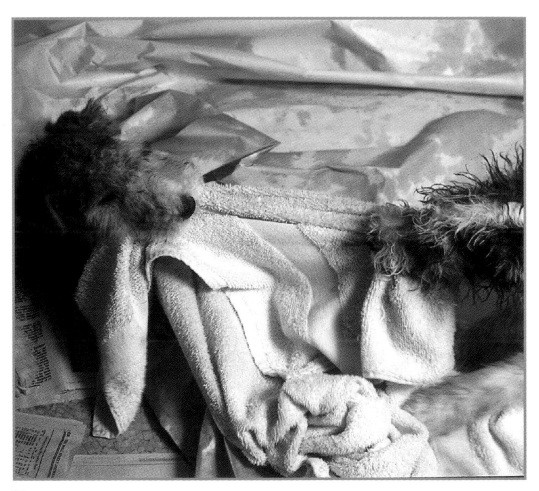

Whether your Wire Fox Terrier becomes a show dog, service dog, participates in obedience or agility trials, or is a companion dog, he will always be the same mischievous puppy you first fell in love with! Rayln Roundelay "Holly", owned by Barbara Gene Bigelow.

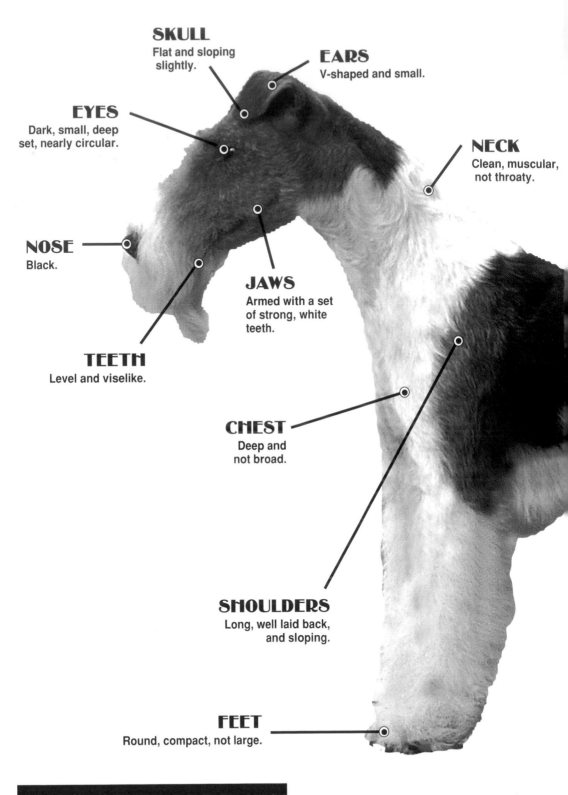

SKULL
Flat and sloping slightly.

EARS
V-shaped and small.

EYES
Dark, small, deep set, nearly circular.

NECK
Clean, muscular, not throaty.

NOSE
Black.

JAWS
Armed with a set of strong, white teeth.

TEETH
Level and viselike.

CHEST
Deep and not broad.

SHOULDERS
Long, well laid back, and sloping.

FEET
Round, compact, not large.

Ch. Random Reaction, owned by W. James and Taffy McFadden.